Exploring John

Everyday Stories

Exploring John

Everyday Stories

Book One

Al W. Adams

LUCAS
PARK
BOOKS

ST. LOUIS, MISSOURI

Table of Contents

Introduction and Welcome!

Bible. Study. These are two words which many (maybe even you) have not been too enthusiastic about. For many, the word 'Bible' is connected with rules and restrictions. Not just that, but what could it possibly have to do with life today? Written thousands of years ago, hasn't it lost its relevance? In a word, no.

And what about the word 'study'? Now there's an exciting word (not)! Let's see, how about the image of long boring hours spent learning things you'll never need? Didn't you leave all that behind when you got out of school?

I want you to try on some new words: experience, explore, and everyday. Let's call them the 'three e's'. What would it be like to experience the Bible texts in your life, right here and now? How about exploring the stories in the setting of your everyday world?

The Exploring...Everyday Stories Bible experience series seeks to help you do just that. You may be someone who has never read the Bible. Maybe you don't even own one! Perhaps you've been in and out of churches all your life, but you've never really connected 'The Book' to your real everyday life. If so, then welcome to the Bible in 'three e's'!

This series is designed to be experienced individually or in groups who are sharing the exploration together. All the Scripture passages are printed in this book, so if you don't own a Bible or yours is hard for you to understand, wait a bit before you purchase one.

You will experience four Bible translations/versions in this exploration journey: (1) The New Revised Standard Version; (2) The New Living Translation; (3) The Contemporary English Version; (4) The Message Version; and (5) The Common English Bible. Each is described in Appendix 1 of this book along with a purchasing source should you decide to buy one or more of them.

In each chapter, you will read a section of Scripture. Most times, it will be presented in two or more translations/versions, so you can experience the 'flavor' of each. Then you will read a true (unless otherwise noted) 'everyday' story related to the Scripture, followed by a connection between the Bible passage and the story. Finally, reflection questions are presented to guide you in further thought and exploration.

Like many of you, I came to a place in my own life where I wondered about the relevance of the Bible to my real, everyday life. Then my eyes were opened as God led me to connect things going on in everyday life with Bible texts. It is my hope and prayer that this exploration experience will lead you to new excitement and growth in your spiritual life. May God richly bless your explorations, may you experience the Holy Spirit in new and powerful ways, and may your eyes be opened to the real presence of Christ in your everyday life!

Rev. Dr. Al W. Adams

1

Stuck Like Glue

In the beginning was the Word, and the Word was with God, and the Word was God. He was in the beginning with God. All things came into being through him, and without him not one thing came into being.
-John 1:1-3, New Revised Standard Version

In the beginning the Word already existed. The Word was with God, and the Word was God. He existed in the beginning with God. God created everything through him, and nothing was created except through him.
-John 1:1-3, New Living Translation

The Word was first, the Word present to God, God present to the Word. The Word was God, in readiness for God from day one. Everything was created through him; nothing--not one thing! - came into being without him.
-John 1:1-3, The Message Version

* * * * * * * * *

"We're stuck with each other – like glue. We're five. We're twins!" That's how I first met Clete and Pete, the "deconstruction team" of the church playground. If you wanted (or didn't) something taken apart, they were your guys. Now I didn't say it would ever go back together the same way again, but they were a good <u>de</u>construction team!

A couple of years went by before I saw them again. Not sure which I was addressing, I simply resorted to a greeting of "Hey!" as one of them came barreling out of the church doors one afternoon. Used to such confusion, the now much taller boy smiled. "Hey! I remember you. I'm Pete. You used to tell on us for fixing the playground stuff. You lived on the corner, right?" I nodded, and he continued almost without drawing a breath. "Well, Clete's here somewhere. We're stuck with each other!"

It was then I noticed something different. Pete was looking at me with his head turned strangely to the right, focusing on me with his left eye. He smiled, and I was immediately embarrassed as I became aware that I was probably giving him an unusual look. "Hey! Here comes Clete now!" And sure enough, Clete came barreling out of the church doors next. Clete's head was tipped strangely to the left, as if he was looking solely out of his right eye.

"Hey! I remember you. You're the tattle-tale lady from when we were little. Well, we're still stuck with each other. We're still twins, and now we're eight!" Clete grinned at his brother as if silently asking him, *Should we tell her?* Pete nodded, and Clete went on. "You know, we've been together from the beginning. We shared everything. Now we're sharing eyes. See, both mine went bad, some disease or something, so Pete gave me one of his. Now we're really stuck together!" Pete playfully punched his brother in the arm. "Yep, I've got the left eye and he's got the right. Together, we've got whole sight!"

He grinned as only an eight year old getting permanent teeth can. Then he winked his left eye, and Clete immediately winked his right. Almost in unison, they said "And they still call us the deconstructors!" And off down the sidewalk they ran.

* * * * * * * * *

Reflections...

Pete and Clete (bet you can't say their names ten times fast!) were indeed together from their beginnings. They needed each other for complete sight, to have complete vision.

So it was with the Living Word and God. All things – all sight, all vision, all reality, all creation – came into being through the Word.

At this beginning of our journey through the Gospel of John, let's think about what it means to be "stuck like glue" with our Creator. When our sight seems nonexistent, we call on God to give us sight, give us understanding, and give us direction. With God, our sight is as complete as humanly possible.

In the grace-filled Gift that was Jesus, God gave us an incredible gift of eternal sight. When our sight was gone, when humankind could no longer see the vision of Creation's purpose, this Living Word became human and came among us.

God, in Jesus, committed to being "stuck like glue" to us. How often do we use the grace-filled sight this holy commitment grants us?

Hear again this Scripture from the Message Version:
The Word was first, the Word present to God, God present to the Word. The Word was God, in readiness for God from day one. Everything was created through him; nothing--not one thing!- came into being without him.
If someone were to look at your life, who and/or what would they think you're "stuck like glue" to?

May you find yourself glued ever more securely to the One who created you.

2

Glow in the Dark

What has come into being in him was life, and the life was the light of all people. **The light shines in the darkness, and the darkness did not overcome it.** *There was a man sent from God, whose name was John.* **He came as a witness to testify to the light, so that all might believe through him.** *He himself was not the light, but he came to testify to the light.*   *-John 1:4-8, New Revised Standard Version*

The Word gave life to everything that was created, and his life brought light to everyone. **The light shines in the darkness, and the darkness can never extinguish it.** *God sent a man, John the Baptist, to* **tell about the light so that everyone might believe** *because of his testimony. John himself was not the light; he was simply a witness to tell about the light.*   *-John 1:4-8, New Living Translation*

What came into existence was Life, and the Life was Light to live by. **The Life-Light blazed out of the darkness; the darkness couldn't put it out.** *There once was a man, his name John, sent by God to* **point out the way to the Life-Light.** *He came to* **show everyone where to look, who to believe in.** *John was not himself the Light; he was there to show the way to the Light.*   *-John 1:4-8, The Message Version*

* * * * * * * * * *

"But bringing Herbie is my homework! The preacher said!"

Who's Herbie? I wondered as I heard the very loud appeal from the direction of the side parking lot one Sunday morning. Even my young son was curious. Looking around me, he pointed at the parent-child Herbie debate taking place as a family got out of their van. **"Mom, who's Herbie and why does that daddy want to lock him in the car?"** My son was clearly curious about what this Herbie kid could have possibly done to deserve locking up in the car. On the other hand, he himself had wanted to stay in our car playing. Maybe he was jealous?

At any rate, I managed to get us heading toward the church building as the parents of the van-family continued the (now louder and more insistent) discussion over the fate of Herbie. Soon my attention was taken by other things as I got my own children settled in their rooms and headed off to teach a youth class.

3

As luck (or fate) would have it, **it was my turn to share the children's message** in worship that morning. As I called the kids up front, the continuation of the Herbie discussion floated through the general rustling of kids moving down the aisles. **"Gimme Herbie. Now!" The young voice was very insistent.** *Just who IS this Herbie,* **I wondered.** I found out soon enough.

Herbie came down the aisle to the front, held securely in the arms of a young girl, her face lit by the glory of winning her "Herbie battle". She mounted the stairs (passing right by me and all the kids gathered on the steps at the front of the sanctuary) and marched right up to the senior pastor.

She plopped Herbie, the big, green stuffed worm right on his lap and proudly announced, **"There! I brought him. Remember me? I'm Heather.** It was real hard, like you said, but you said we were supposed to glow for Jesus, and like I told you, **Herbie's got to know Jesus,** because he glows real bright – his whole face glows in the dark!"

I could tell Rev. Mike was having a hard time. First, he seemed to be valiantly trying to remember the connection a big, green, glow-in-the-dark stuffed worm could possibly have to last week's sermon message. Second, he was really struggling to keep a straight face. Finally, as his eyes met mine, I knew **he was trying to figure out what to do now!**

Kids are pretty smart, and eerily observant (especially when grownups need more time to think). She placed her hands on her hips, leaned into Rev Mike's lapel microphone, and said, "Well, he's here. He's got to gather light, 'cause then he stores it up so he can shine it out on everyone. My mom and dad, they wanted to lock Herbie in our van, but I knew you'd want him in here so he could gather up some Jesus-light and go shine it on my friends who don't know Him, right?" Before Rev Mike could think of a response, she went on.

"I brought my friend Masie today. She met Herbie and wanted to see where he got his light. I told her it was Jesus, and she wants to meet Him. Can she meet Him here? Can she right now? She's sitting right there." She pointed out her new friend, who was sitting among the children on the steps with me.

Rev Mike looked at me. I looked at him. And the sermon message changed right then. He came down with young Heather and sat on the steps in the midst of those kids. He came to meet Masie. **That day Herbie introduced some children (and a lot of grown-ups) to the light of Christ.**

* * * * * * * * *

Reflections...

That day, Heather *"came as a witness to testify to the light, so that all might believe through"... her.* How about us? No matter the darkness around us, we can come into His presence to gather light as we worship, study, fellowship, and serve together in His name. No matter the obstacles, Christ will light us up and give us incredible strength and creativity to witness to the eternal Light that is our Lord and Savior.

How about us? How are we following Heather's example? How many "Masie's" are we bringing His light to?

3

Pitch That Tent!

*The true light that shines on everyone was coming into the world. The Word was in the world, but no one knew him, though God had made the world with his Word. He came into his own world, but his own nation did not welcome him. Yet some people accepted him and put their faith in him. So he gave them the right to be the children of God. They were not God's children by nature or because of any human desires. God himself was the one who made them his children. **The Word became a human being and lived here with us.** We saw his true glory, the glory of the only Son of the Father. From him all the kindness and all the truth of God have come down to us.*

-John 1:9-14, Contemporary English Version

The Life-Light was the real thing: **Every person entering Life he brings into Light.** *He was in the world, the world was there through him, and yet the world didn't even notice. He came to his own people, but they didn't want him. But whoever did want him, who believed he was who he claimed and would do what he said, He made to be their true selves, their child-of-God selves. These are the God-begotten, not blood-begotten, not flesh-begotten, not sex-begotten.* **The Word became flesh and blood, and moved into the neighborhood.** *We saw the glory with our own eyes, the one-of-a-kind glory, like Father, like Son, Generous inside and out, true from start to finish.*

-John 1:9-14, The Message Version

* * * * * * * * *

"I've got a play for our Christmas program, Miss Linda! I wrote it myself!" Shelly could hardly contain herself. It was the first gathering of children and youth to plan parts for the upcoming Christmas program. "Miss Linda" had **already met with the pastor and together they'd selected the program.** She'd called on volunteer adults to help with building the set (Bethlehem, of course), getting the costumes together (Biblical time period costumes, of course), and thinking through which young person might be best for each role (Mary, Joseph, Baby Jesus, shepherds, etc., of course).

"That's nice, Shelly. But you know we've already got the play picked out for this year, honey. **Maybe we could look at it for next year, OK?"** At that response, eight year old Shelly's face scrunched into a fierce frown. "But Miss Linda, **don't we want Jesus to come HERE this Christmas?** He always comes to Beth-lee-hem, but when my grandpa read the Bible story last week, he told me John (I think he's Jesus' best friend) **really said Jesus moved into OUR neighborhood** when He came from heaven. Grandpa and me, we built a 'Jesus-tent' right in our yard. **It's got a Jesus-cradle bed AND a cross too! 'Cause that's why He came, right Miss Linda?"**

"Sure, Shelly. But that's what our Christmas program's all about every year too. Jesus coming right here to earth." Linda began to shuffle papers and get people's attention so the (now late) planning and practice meeting could begin. **Not to be turned down so easily,** as soon as the room got quiet, Shelly cleared her throat (loudly). "But **what if Jesus pitched his tent at the grocery store?** What then? Or maybe where my mom works, or on the soccer field where my brother plays? What then?"

Instant conversation. Instant loss of control for Linda. **Soon everyone from the youngest child to the oldest adult was discussing the possibilities.** What if Jesus pitched a tent at the post office? In the middle of the mall? In the airport? The potential tent-pitching locations were endless! Linda pulled Shelly aside. "OK Shelly," she began, with a smile tugging at the corners of her mouth, "What do you have in mind?"

Shelly straightened up to the tallest three-foot-eight she could muster. "Well, we could do what I did to write this..." Shelly held out a neatly handwritten script. "This is what my grandpa, my brother, and me wrote for our family. We could do the same thing for our church. It'd be so much fun!"

That's how the unique Christmas program "Jesus on Location" began. It was a series of short scenes depicting what might happen if Jesus really did "pitch His tent" in these modern everyday places. They ended up performing the play in at least eight neighboring churches in addition to their own as requests came pouring in. At last count, there were churches in six states who had adapted the idea for their own Christmas programs.

* * * * * * * * *

Reflections...

The Greek word that is translated as "lived here with us" or "moved into the neighborhood" is "skhno" (pronounced skay-no') and **literally means "to pitch one's tent among".**

What would it be like to have Jesus literally "pitch His tent" in your neighborhood?

In your front yard?

Where you work, play, or go to school?

Reflections (continued)

How about in the grocery store parking lot?

How would you describe the impact?

You may be thinking this is a one time a year kind of thing, like those Christmas decorations. In fact, if you're reading this in, say, July, you might have been tempted to skip this chapter altogether.

I'm really glad you didn't, because **Scripture doesn't say Jesus "pitched his tent" for a few days and then left.** Not at all. In fact, Jesus Himself tells us that "Whenever two or more are gathered in my name, there I am in the midst of them."(Mt 18:20) Jesus came that His Presence might transform the world!

My prayer for you is that you allow Jesus the Christ to "pitch His tent" in your life – everywhere you go, and in every company you keep.

4

Holy Hearing Aids

(John testified to him and cried out, **"This was he of whom I said,** *'He who comes after me ranks ahead of me because he was before me.'")* *From his fullness we have all received, grace upon grace. The law indeed was given through Moses; grace and truth came through Jesus Christ. No one has ever seen God. It is God the only Son, who is close to the Father's heart, who has made him known.*

This is the testimony given by John when the Jews sent priests and Levites from Jerusalem to ask him, "Who are you?" He confessed and did not deny it, *but confessed, "I am not the Messiah." And they asked him, "What then? Are you Elijah?" He said, "I am not." "Are you the prophet?" He answered, "No."*

Then they said to him, "Who are you? Let us have an answer for those who sent us. What do you say about yourself?" He said, **"I am the voice of one crying out in the wilderness, 'Make straight the way of the Lord,'"** *as the* **prophet Isaiah said.**

Now they had been sent from the Pharisees. They asked him, "Why then are you baptizing if you are neither the Messiah, nor Elijah, nor the prophet?"

John answered them, "I baptize with water. Among you stands one whom you do not know, the one who is coming after me; I am not worthy to untie the thong of his sandal." This took place in Bethany across the Jordan where John was baptizing. -John 1:15-28, New Revised Standard Version

John pointed him out and called, **"This is the One! The One I told you was coming** *after me but in fact was ahead of me. He has always been ahead of me, has always had the first word." We all live off his generous bounty, gift after gift after gift. We got the basics from Moses, and then this exuberant giving and receiving, This endless knowing and understanding - all this came through Jesus, the Messiah. No one has ever seen God, not so much as a glimpse. This one-of-a-kind God-Expression, who exists at the very heart of the Father, has made him plain as day.*

When Jews from Jerusalem sent a group of priests and officials to ask John who he was, he was completely honest. He didn't evade the question. He told the plain truth: *"I am not the Messiah." They pressed him, "Who, then? Elijah?" "I am not." "The Prophet?" "No."*

Exasperated, they said, "Who, then? We need an answer for those who sent us. Tell us something - anything! - about yourself." "I'm thunder in the desert: 'Make the road straight for God!' **I'm doing what the prophet Isaiah preached."**

Those sent to question him were from the Pharisee party. Now they had a question of their own: "If you're neither the Messiah, nor Elijah, nor the Prophet, why do you baptize?"

John answered, "I only baptize using water. A person you don't recognize has taken his stand in your midst. He comes after me, but he is not in second place to me. I'm not even worthy to hold his coat for him." These conversations took place in Bethany on the other side of the Jordan, where John was baptizing at the time.

-John 1:15-28, The Message Version

* * * * * * * * *

"I TOLD you, the FISH is BURNING!!" Exasperation dripped from his voice as Fred entered the family room where Leslie sat reading the paper. Looking up, she responded, "What? What's churning? What wish are you talking about?" He shook his head and smiled. *Wish she'd get her hearing checked....*

"Well, honey, I've said it three times. Guess I need to be closer. I said...the fish is burning. I've turned off the stove and turned the fans on now, so we can go out for dinner. Ready?" Fred picked up his jacket, Leslie nodded and put shoes on, and they left for the corner grill. As they sat in the restaurant later, she wondered, ***Do I need hearing aids?***

* * * * * * * * *

"Mom, I really thought I'd told you about the cast party. I wrote it on the kitchen calendar and everything. You even asked me where it was, who was going, and all that, on the way to play practice last week. So can I go?" Lately Carla wondered if her mom heard anything. She could feel the stress just rolling off mom ever since grandma died. Mom was the only daughter, so she'd had to "take care of everything". Wow. Carla never knew "everything" could be so big or hurt so much. She looked across grandma's kitchen at her mom, waiting for an answer. Maybe if they got back to church. Mom had friends there – good friends who'd support her, maybe even help her get some of her "hearing" back....

Leslie thought.....*How could I not have heard Carla?* **How could I not remember?** *Carla had always been good about planning and asking permission. In fact, Carla was the queen of organization! I know she got that from her dad. Wish he was still here...* But cancer had taken him away from them three years ago. Now it was just the two of them. *How could I have missed this?* **How could I not have heard? Maybe I need to have my hearing checked....**

* * * * * * * * *

Reflections...

Can you step into John's shoes for a minute? Hear his possible thoughts: *I've told them! How can they not get it? It's in the prophecy – and everyone knows that! I mean, really – Isaiah told us – Isaiah! How many times do I have to tell them before they finally get it?*

Reflections (continued)

How would you answer John? I mean, really?

Maybe you'd suggest they get their spiritual hearing checked. Perhaps some…well, some "holy hearing aids" would help. They did seem to need a bit of help tuning in to the reality of what John was saying and tuning out a bit (or more) of the world's many competing voices.

What about us? Jesus makes Himself known all around us, every day, in so many ways. Are we tuned in? Do we have our "holy hearing aids" turned on?

My prayer for you is that you turn up your "holy hearing aids"– everywhere you go, and in every company you keep.

5

100 Proof!

*The next day John saw Jesus coming toward him and said, "**Look!** The Lamb of God who takes away the sin of the world! **He is the one I was talking about** when I said, 'A man is coming after me who is far greater than I am, for he existed long before me.' I did not recognize him as the Messiah, but I have been baptizing with water so that he might be revealed to Israel."*

*Then John testified, "I saw the Holy Spirit descending like a dove from heaven and resting upon him. I didn't know he was the one, but when God sent me to baptize with water, he told me, 'The one on whom you see the Spirit descend and rest is the one who will baptize with the Holy Spirit.' **I saw this happen to Jesus, so I testify that he is the Chosen One of God."***   *-John 1:29-34, New Living Translation*

*The very next day John saw Jesus coming toward him and yelled out, "**Here he is,** God's Passover Lamb! He forgives the sins of the world! **This is the man I've been talking about,** "the One who comes after me but is really ahead of me.' I knew nothing about who he was--only this: that my task has been to get Israel ready to recognize him as the God-Revealer. That is why I came here baptizing with water, giving you a good bath and scrubbing sins from your life so you can get a fresh start with God."*

*John clinched his witness with this: "I watched the Spirit, like a dove flying down out of the sky, making himself at home in him. I repeat, I know nothing about him except this: The One who authorized me to baptize with water told me, "The One on whom you see the Spirit come down and stay, this One will baptize with the Holy Spirit.' **That's exactly what I saw happen, and I'm telling you, there's no question about it: This is the Son of God."***   *-John 1:29-34, The Message Version*

* * * * * * * * *

"This church stuff...it's REAL hundred-proof, man!"

What? What IS this guy talking about – and at an AA meeting, no less!

Seeing my (probably very obvious) look of confusion and dismay, the meeting leader laughed. "OK, Jerry, you'd better explain to the good reverend here, else she'll really wonder!"

The table got quiet. Almost too quiet. I could tell this was serious stuff as Jerry cleared his throat and paused before speaking. "Well, you see it's like this: I started when I was about, oh, six, nipping bits from my

11

granddad's drinks. Rum and Coke, that was his "evening tonic". Don't know that he ever caught on, but pretty soon I figured out where the liquor was. You know, lotta Coke, little rum, then less Coke, more rum – you get it. That's how it went for a number of years, till I was sixteen."

"One day when my older brother came home from the navy…well, he caught me in the liquor cabinet up above the refrigerator. 'Bout knocked me clean off that stool (it was behind the kitchen door). I couldn't never lie to my big brother anyway. I thought I was in big trouble, but you know what? Bill, he just grabbed another stool and climbed right up there with me. Told me this stuff ain't nothin', why he's had hundred proof liquor! Proof? I said…what's that? So he explained it to me, right there on them stools in that kitchen. 'Why, little brother, hundred proof's 'bout as good as it gets!' Oh yeah. Well, you know I'm here tonight, so you know I can tell you it's a hundred alright – a hundred percent trouble!"

Jerry looked around the table, enjoying the telling of a story I knew he'd told before (from the looks that seemed to be waiting for the 'rest of the story'). "OK, OK, I'm getting to the real stuff. So anyway, I don't remember much between sixteen and forty. What I do remember is this guy coming around on the streets bringing blankets and sandwiches, soup and cookies, - and talking about this **Jesus guy who turned water into wine. Now THAT was a guy I had to meet!"**

General laughter greeted that last comment, but I could tell by the crack in Jerry's voice that bigger stuff was coming. As the table got quiet again, he continued. **"A forty year old walking dead guy – that's what I was. And this guy wanted to introduce me to this Jesus, who could give me more wine?** By then, even I knew more wine was more trouble! Know what else this guy said? He told me, plain as day, 'Oh, yeah, Jesus knows about trouble all right. Nothing he hasn't heard.' Well, **I just had to meet this Jesus!**

This guy'd been coming around oh, maybe a month or so when I finally dared him to take me to meet Jesus. He'd been telling me about Jesus for so long, I thought maybe I was imagining things (did that a lot in those days). I'll never forget that day. May 19, 1994 it was, round about supper time. The guy came around with one of his friends to pick me up and take me to meet this Jesus. **Never knew God like that.**

Never knew Jesus was a real guy, like me. Well, not quite like me maybe, but close enough. That day, now THAT was a hundred-proof day! I met the real thing to last me all my life that day. Ain't never forgot it, and I ain't likely to either. Yep, **Jesus is pure hundred-proof stuff!"**

* * * * * * * * * *

Reflections…

Jerry filled his life with alcohol and the "street life", as he called it. We probably fill our lives with other things. Lots of those things command our attention, and before long those things may take the "hundred-proof" place in our lives.

What's the "real-est real thing" in your life?

Reflections (continued)

Could you testify about it? Is it worthy of the place in your life you've granted it?

John the Baptist is calling the people to see and claim Christ as Messiah. He's introducing Him to them in the midst of their lives. He's calling them to place Him as the "100-proof", "good as it gets" priority in their lives. Will they do it? Will we?

Will we, like the man who introduced Jesus to Jerry, be ready to show Him to others? He really is our "100-proof", "good as it gets" Savior!

6

Now?

The next day John again was standing with two of his disciples, and as he watched Jesus walk by, he exclaimed, "Look, here is the Lamb of God!"

The two disciples heard him say this, and they followed Jesus.

When Jesus turned and saw them following, he said to them, "What are you looking for?" They said to him, "Rabbi" (which translated means Teacher), "where are you staying?"

He said to them, "Come and see." They came and saw *where he was staying, and they remained with him that day. It was about four o'clock in the afternoon.*

One of the two who heard John speak and followed him was Andrew, Simon Peter's brother. He first found his brother Simon and said to him, "We have found the Messiah" (which is translated Anointed).

He brought Simon to Jesus, *who looked at him and said, "You are Simon son of John. You are to be called Cephas"*
(which is translated Peter). - John 1:35-42, New Revised Standard Version

The next day John was standing again with two of his disciples. When he saw Jesus walking along he said, "Look! The Lamb of God!"

The two disciples heard what he said, and they followed Jesus.

When Jesus turned and saw them following, he asked, "What are you looking for?" They said, "Rabbi (which is translated Teacher), where are you staying?"

He replied, "Come and see." So they went and saw *where he was staying, and they remained with him that day. It was about four o'clock in the afternoon.*

One of the two disciples who heard what John said and followed Jesus was Andrew, the brother of Simon Peter. He first found his own brother Simon and said to him, "We have found the Messiah" (which is translated Christ).

He led him to Jesus. *Jesus looked at him and said, "You are Simon, son of John. You will be called Cephas" (which is translated Peter).* - John 1:35-42, Common English Bible

* * * * * * * * *

The lot had been empty for over ten years, ever since the horrific fire had burned it to the ground. The news media had called it a "freak accident" when the driver of an eighteen wheeler lost control of his rig and plowed through the tiny one bedroom home on the corner. Then they'd switched gears completely, calling the survival of the homeowner, ninety year old "Grandma Mary", a miracle. **As the semi literally blew through her home, she had been driven into her back yard while asleep in her bed.**

Then, as she barely began to comprehend what happened, what was left of her home erupted in a ball of fire. When the fire department finished, a pile of ashes and debris was all that remained. She gave the lot to the local Habitat for Humanity organization and took her heavy oak bed with her when she went to live with her granddaughter in a nearby town. And so the small corner lot sat. Seasons came and went. Grass and weeds grew, mowed occasionally by the city or charitable neighbors. **Then one day…..**

When her doorbell rang, Wanda looked out her window. *Oh no. A guy with a clipboard. Probably another sales or survey guy.* Unfortunately, the only way to get to her car and the grocery store was out the front door, right past this guy. *Might as well get it over with.*

As she opened her front door, Wanda noticed he wore a "Habitat for Humanity" name tag. Hmmm. Interesting. "How can I help you, young man. I'm in a hurry right now, on my way to the grocery."

"My name's Tad, ma'am, and I'll only take a minute. **We're looking to build a house on the corner** down the street, and we're talking to neighbors like yourself to see what you think."

"What I think is, it's about time! You know Grandma Mary used to live there, but she's gone home to Jesus 'bout five years ago now." Wanda put her bag down in the house and invited Tad to sit with her on the porch as she launched into the story of "Grandma Mary's midnight ride" as the story had become known in the neighborhood. "Wow!" was all Tad could find to say, especially when he realized the story was true.

"So, you're finally here to build a house?" Wanda peered at Tad over her glasses. "No ma'am. I'm just letting folks know about the house that's coming, that's all."

"Now? Is it coming now?" Wanda asked as she stood and picked up her bag. "Soon. Very soon you should see work begin." Seeing the hope in Wanda's eyes, Tad wished he could build the house right then.

The next day, Wanda went to the neighborhood meeting. The president announced with great excitement that she'd seen the "Habitat construction boss" on the corner lot just that morning. "Yes indeed," she said, "and he was poking around like he was planning something too!"

Wanda raised her hand. **"Now?" she asked, "or when?"** Nobody seemed to know.

So Wanda began to keep her eyes open. Morning and night she took her dog for his walk past the corner lot. Just two days later there it was – a truck with the Habitat for Humanity logo on the side! She stopped to introduce herself. The friendly young man told her construction would begin…now! She almost couldn't believe her ears.

"Now?," she asked. "Really, NOW?" As the man nodded yes, she bounced with excitement. "You know, I didn't think I'd live to see Grandma Mary's dream come true, and now, I'm so excited!" Wanda hurried home, sharing the news with neighbors she saw on her way.

"Now!," she exclaimed, "The time is now! They're starting the home-building NOW!"

✳ ✳ ✳ ✳ ✳ ✳ ✳ ✳ ✳

Let's take a short trip back to review what brings us to the Scripture for this chapter. At the start of this Gospel, in answer to the priests and Levites (sent by the Pharisees) asking who he is, John announces that the Messiah is coming. **Coming. Not now, but coming.** Nope, I'm not Him.

Not satisfied with John's answer, they asked again: "What do you say about yourself?" (v. 22) They needed an answer! "I am the voice of one crying in the wilderness," he told them. You can imagine how confused they might have been. They may have been thinking, *What IS this guy talking about?*

So John went down to the Jordan River to testify, teach, and baptize. Among the crowd coming to be baptized one day was…Him…the Messiah Himself! The next day as John reported the events of the day (vv. 29-24) he related something utterly amazing: the Holy Spirit of God visibly appeared from heaven, landed on this Messiah, Jesus, and a voice from heaven proclaimed Him. **The time is here – now!**

Like Wanda and her neighbors, people are waiting. They have differing motivations, some good, some not. But they all are asking, **"Now? Is it now? Is this it?"** And finally, finally the answer is… **Yes!**

In this chapter's Gospel text, we listen in as John is with two of his followers and Jesus, the Messiah Himself, walks by. **"There He is!"** John's disciples immediately step into the "now" as they leave John to follow Jesus, who turns and asks them what they're looking for. In other words, **are they sure they really want to step into the "now" of the arrival of the Messiah?** There is a vast difference in waiting for something and stepping fully into its arrival; it's the action step. It is moving from dreaming, preparing, and fashioning "when it happens" scenarios to actually stepping into action and participating in the Now! time.

Much like Wanda, these two disciples were fully committed. They didn't need to answer Jesus' question. They knew what they were seeking – the Messiah. They knew what they had found – the Messiah. What they wanted was to know: "Where are you staying?" **They were ready to move into action!** Wanda knew what she was looking for, and she knew it when she found it.

Andrew, one of those two disciples, went into action. He told his brother Simon. But he didn't stop there. He brought Simon to Jesus. You can almost guess the conversation. **"Yes, NOW! The Messiah is here NOW! Come and see!"** And not just the neighborhood, but the world, would never be the same.

Wanda started telling people, everywhere she went – the grocery, the bus stop, the beauty shop – everywhere. **"Now!"**, she said with excitement, **"Now! It's happening; come and see for yourself!"** Word spread throughout the neighborhood and the community around it. The home was built. A single dad with four boys moved in, and he placed a welcome sign in the front garden. It said, "Welcome to Grandma Mary's Miracle House!".

The word of the Messiah's presence in the world has spread down through the ages. From John, to those two disciples, to you and I: the time is now. **Yes, NOW! The instruction? Come and see! Go, and tell!**

* * * * * * * * *

Reflections...

Many times, we are afraid to act until we have all the information about something. Sometimes, this is very wise. Think of a time when getting all the information possible before making a decision was a very smart thing to do. What did you do?

Now, think about your faith life. Are you waiting for all the information before you step into action in your life of discipleship? Are you stuck in the "land of waiting", afraid to admit that the time is indeed now? What will you do next?

Here's the thing: the Messiah has come! He walks beside you, persistently telling YOU: "Come and see!" See what your life could be like as my disciple in action. See how your life will be made new each and every day as you walk with Me."

And you can't help yourself. You turn to Him and ask, **"Now? Do you mean NOW?"**

He smiles. **"Yes, my child, my potential disciple....NOW! Let's GO!"**

What would you do first?

7

Invisible Sight

The next day Jesus decided to go to Galilee. He found Philip and said to him, "Follow me."

Now Philip was from Bethsaida, the city of Andrew and Peter. Philip found Nathanael and said to him, "We have found him about whom Moses in the law and also the prophets wrote, Jesus son of Joseph from Nazareth."

Nathanael said to him, "Can anything good come out of Nazareth?" Philip said to him, "Come and see."

When Jesus saw Nathanael coming toward him, he said of him, "Here is truly an Israelite in whom there is no deceit!"

Nathanael asked him, "Where did you get to know me?" Jesus answered, "I saw you under the fig tree before Philip called you."

Nathanael replied, "Rabbi, you are the Son of God! You are the King of Israel!"

Jesus answered, "Do you believe because I told you that I saw you under the fig tree? You will see greater things than these." And he said to him, "Very truly, I tell you, you will see heaven opened and the angels of God ascending and descending upon the Son of Man."   *- John 1:43-51, New Revised Standard Version*

The next day Jesus decided to go to Galilee. When He got there, He ran across Philip and said, "Come, follow me." (Philip's hometown was Bethsaida, the same as Andrew and Peter.)

Philip went and found Nathanael and told him, "We've found the One Moses wrote of in the Law, the One preached by the prophets. It's Jesus, Joseph's son, the one from Nazareth!"

"Nazareth? You've got to be kidding." But Philip said, "Come, see for yourself."

When Jesus saw him coming, He said, "There's a real Israelite, not a false bone in his body." Nathanael said, "Where did you get that idea? You don't know me."

Jesus answered, "One day, long before Philip called you here, I saw you under the fig tree." Nathanael exclaimed, "Rabbi! You are the Son of God, the King of Israel!"

Jesus said, "You've become a believer simply because I say I saw you one day sitting under the fig tree? You haven't seen anything yet! Before this is over you're going to see heaven open and God's angels descending to the Son of Man and ascending again."   *- John 1:43-51, The Message Version*

* * * * * * * * *

When I first met Jim in college, it unnerved and puzzled me. "Well, let me see...", he would start out. Or maybe, "Well, if you just look over there,...." We were in the same undergrad zoology lab course. Common lab tools included microscopes, organism diagrams, and organ system function charts. **Here's the thing: Jim was blind. As in totally.**

Now imagine a guide dog named Cap in a zoology lab. Cap was fascinated by all the sights, sounds, and especially smells. You could see it in his eyes as he sat by Jim's side or lay under the lab table. Nose twitching and analyzing it all – **he loved zoology!**

One day, our team was hard at work on a dissection project, locating and diagramming frog organs and parts. The puzzle? We'd been told that our frog had an anomaly (abnormal feature) and our task was to find it. An hour into the task, having no success, and quickly approaching our time deadline, Jim spoke up. "Try looking behind and to the right of the intestine. From what I can see, it looks like this little guy probably has a tumor somewhere around there."

What? The rest of us had gone over that frog at least ten times! But....**Jim was absolutely correct.** The small tumor was right where he thought it was! Unable to contain myself, I blurted out, **"From what you can SEE? How did you know?"** Jim shrugged. "Well," he said, "first the position of the legs, then the way everything was situated as all of you described it...I just knew, that's all."

We finished the lab project with about three minutes to spare. As Jim and I cleaned up our work station (we drew clean-up duty that day), **I was still trying to figure out how Jim's "sight" worked.** "So Jim, can you see shadows, or....?" He laughed. Cap sat up straight, eyes glued on Jim.

"You might say I have 'invisible sight'. I just see differently. People sometimes assume I don't know, can't see, basically that I'm helpless. Actually, I have a bit of fun every time I surprise someone with my ability to see. I map things in my head, and I listen carefully, a lot like Cap here does when he's trying to figure me out and predict what I'm about to do. Most times, I can even tell if somebody's telling me the truth or not."

All I could think of in response was an amazed "wow". Jim invited me to join him and Cap for a walk to the local coffee shop. As we walked, he described the scenery we passed pretty accurately. I found myself more and more awed at his "invisible sight".

We got our drinks and sat down. **"Know the real reason I call it 'invisible sight'?** It has nothing to do with what I've just shown you. **It has everything to do with seeing God.** I've never had human eyes to do that, and yet especially when I pray, I can smell heaven and I can see God with my whole being. **You might say that being blind helps me see.** It's pretty radical!"

$$* * * * * * * * * *$$

Second Corinthians 5:6-7 tells us, *"So we are always confident....for we walk by faith, not by sight."* We are so much like Nathanael in the selection from John's Gospel above. We see what we see...with our human eyes. In fact, what we humanly see tempts us to act as if that's all there is to see! Many times it takes so little to convince us that something is real, important, and reliable.

Nathanael was challenged by Jesus to look for God's amazing presence and power beyond human sight – into heaven itself! Jesus told him that beyond mere human sight he would see angels tending to and accompanying Jesus ("ascending and descending upon"). Jesus was teaching Nathanael to be discerning, to use what my friend Jim would call "invisible sight", enabled and powered by God, to decide what was proof and work of Jesus the Messiah and what was not.

Jim was correct: Jesus was, and is, radical. When Paul instructed those in the early church to "walk by faith and not by sight", he taught them that **heavenly sight could be trusted to guide us to eternity with the Lord.** Paul's human eyes had to be literally blinded before he could see the reality of Christ (see Acts 9). **Once he had experienced Christ, his life was never the same.**

* * * * * * * * *

Reflections...

Like Philip and Nathanael, like Paul and faithful Christ-followers before us, we must work on enlarging our sight as well. We must intentionally enlarge our sight beyond what our physical eyes can see. We must train ourselves to look for God's presence with our whole being.

How would you describe the state of your "invisible sight"?

When you are with others, when you are making decisions, when you are building relationships....how do YOU see?

8

The Resurrection of Last Place

On the third day there was a wedding in Cana of Galilee, and the mother of Jesus was there. Jesus and His disciples had also been invited to the wedding. When the wine gave out, the mother of Jesus said to Him, "They have no wine." And Jesus said to her, "Woman, what concern is that to you and to me? My hour has not yet come."

His mother said to the servants, "Do whatever He tells you." Now standing there were six stone water jars for the Jewish rites of purification, each holding twenty or thirty gallons. Jesus said to them, "Fill the jars with water." And they filled them up to the brim. He said to them, "Now draw some out, and take it to the chief steward." So they took it.

*When the steward tasted the water that had become wine, and did not know where it had come from (though the servants who had drawn the water knew), the steward called the bridegroom and said to him, **"Everyone serves the good wine first, and then the inferior wine after the guests have become drunk. But you have kept the good wine until now."***

Jesus did this, the first of His signs, in Cana of Galilee, and revealed His glory; and His disciples believed in Him.
*   - John 2:1-11, New Revised Standard Version*

Three days later there was a wedding in the village of Cana in Galilee. Jesus' mother was there. Jesus and His disciples were guests also. When they started running low on wine at the wedding banquet, Jesus' mother told Him, "They're just about out of wine." Jesus said, "Is that any or our business, Mother – yours or mine? This isn't my time. Don't push me,"

She went ahead anyway, telling the servants, "Whatever He tells you, do it." Six stoneware water pots were there, used by the Jews for ritual washings. Each held twenty to thirty gallons. Jesus ordered the servants, "Fill the pots with water." And they filled them to the brim. "Now fill your pitchers and take them to the host," Jesus said, and they did.

*When the host tasted the water that had become wine (he didn't know what had just happened but the servants, of course, knew), he called out to the bridegroom, **"Everybody I know begins with their finest wines and after the guests have had their fill brings in the cheap stuff. But you've saved the best till now!"***

This act in Cana of Galilee was the first sign Jesus gave, the first glimpse of His glory. And His disciples believed in Him.
*   - John 2:1-11, The Message Version*

* * * * * * * * * *

"We're counting on you to win this thing for us, Barry." *Was coach completely crazy?* When the other three runners on the relay team had come up sick or injured, Barry thought for sure they'd just default the race. I mean, really – this was the state championship semi-final relay race! Besides, Barry usually ran first, so the other runners after him could make up the time he'd lost.

Was coach completely crazy? Lost in his panicked thoughts, the next thing he heard coach say was, "Yeah, Barry, I need you to run last, in the anchor spot. I know you can do it. Besides, I've had to pull the others from the alternate list. You're faster than them. **I'm counting on you to bring this thing home for us."**

Was coach completely crazy? Now he was beginning to feel more than a little sick himself. Already a sophomore running on the varsity team, now he'd be up against much more experienced opponents. How would he; how could he – compete with them?

As time for the race drew near, Barry gathered with his new relay teammates. As they looked around at the competition, Trent, who would run first, commented, "Well, looks like they saved the best for last, huh?" Barry looked over at the sidelines and caught the eye of his coach. It was then that inspiration took over.

"I think you've got it dead right, Trent. You know what? We've got it in us too. Maybe we'll shock 'em all. Yeah, **I think this is the day that what everyone thinks is last place comes in first.** This is our chance."

Well, after Trent ran the first leg of the race, they were a little behind (OK, fourth out of six). After the second runner, they were a bit more behind (fifth out of sixth and fading fast). When the third runner came around the track to pass off the runner's baton to Barry, well, let's just say they were in last place and fading – really fast.

Was coach completely crazy? Barry glanced at his teammates at the moment he grabbed the baton and began his leg of the race – the anchor leg. It was then that the inspiration left his mouth and entered his legs. He ran like he'd never run before. As Barry rounded the track, he counted the runners he passed. One, two, three, four....unbelievable! They finished tied for first place!

Shaking Barry's hand after the race, the coach of the tying first place team shook his head in amazement. **"Son, seems like your coach saved the best for last. I've seen you run – never knew you had THAT in you!"**

* * * * * * * * *

Many times we simply don't know the amount of grace and power God has placed within us – until it comes out in the most surprising ways! We judge ourselves to be like "just plain water", or worse, the "cheap wine" in the Scripture story we just read.

Sometimes, we look at our friends, neighbors, and those we're "running the race" of life with, and we **find ourselves giving up, blind to the amazing possibilities** God has created in us and the amazing things God can do through us!

Three of the four Gospels bring this miracle of Jesus to life in a new way. Jesus says this: *"But many who are first will be last, and the last will be first."* (Mk. 10:31, Lk. 13:30, Mt. 19:30) Likewise, **Christ is crucified, exhibited as one of the "least and last", a criminal, not worthy of living. God raised and resurrected Him to sit at God's right hand – in first place!**

So it is in our lives when we decide to follow Christ. We experience over and over again the incredible power of the "resurrection of last place."

* * * * * * * * *

Reflections...

What areas of your life occupy "last place", where you have lost hope of success (your "plain water" zones)?

What would those areas be like if God's resurrection power entered them (and they became like the "finest wine" in your life)?

What do the words "resurrection of last place" mean to you?

9

Holy Renovation

After this he went down to Capernaum with his mother, his brothers, and his disciples; and they remained there a few days. The Passover of the Jews was near, and Jesus went up to Jerusalem. In the temple he found people selling cattle, sheep, and doves, and the money changers seated at their tables.

Making a whip of cords, he drove all of them out of the temple, both the sheep and the cattle. He also poured out the coins of the money changers and overturned their tables. He told those who were selling the doves, "Take these things out of here! Stop making my Father's house a marketplace!" His disciples remembered that it was written, "Zeal for your house will consume me."

*The Jews then said to him, "What sign can you show us for doing this?" Jesus answered them, **"Destroy this temple, and in three days I will raise it up."***

The Jews then said, "This temple has been under construction for forty-six years, and will you raise it up in three days?"

But he was speaking of the temple of his body. After he was raised from the dead, his disciples remembered that he had said this; and they believed the scripture and the word that Jesus had spoken.

- John 2:12-22, New Revised Standard Version

After this, Jesus and His mother, His brothers, and His disciples went down to Capernaum and stayed there a few days. It was nearly time for the Jewish Passover, and Jesus went up to Jerusalem. He found in the temple those who were selling cattle, sheep, and doves, as well as those involved in exchanging currency sitting there.

He made a whip from ropes and chased them all out of the temple, including the cattle and the sheep. He scattered the coins and overturned the tables of those who exchanged currency. He said to the dove sellers, "Get these things out of here! Don't make my Father's house a place of business." His disciples remembered that it is written, 'Passion for your house consumes me.'

*Then the Jewish leaders asked Him, "By what authority are You doing these things? What miraculous sign will You show us?" Jesus answered, **"Destroy this temple and in three days I'll raise it up."***

The Jewish leaders replied, "It took forty-six years to build this temple, and You will raise it up in three days?" But the temple Jesus was talking about was His body. After He was raise from the dead, His disciples remembered what He had said, and they believed the Scripture and the word that Jesus had spoken.

- John 2:12-22, Common English Bible

* * * * * * * * * *

(Note: All names in the following true story have been changed to protect privacy)

It was a place of safety. The Edson Home was a refuge for children ages ten to sixteen who had been removed from their homes due to abuse and/or neglect issues.

It was a place of security. Locked, alarmed doors, check-in and check-out procedures carefully and completely followed, and lists of approved (and specifically unapproved) visitors followed very carefully.

It was a place of healing. Attitudes of calm, caring, respect, and positive life direction were priorities in all aspects of life at The Edson Home. Protecting and healing these young lives was the paramount purpose for its very existence.

One of the activities offered twice each week was a time of Bible study and simple worship. So five young people gathered in the "common area" to read and talk about the above Scripture one Wednesday afternoon.

"Man, I can just see Jesus cleaning MY old house that way! Whoa baby, animals in MY house looked a lot different from those cows and stuff." Thirteen year old Addy had been rescued from a home where she was locked in and sold repeatedly to fund her stepdad's drug habits.

"Yeah, I get that one, for sure. But you know what? **The day the cops came and raided my old house? They were just like that, only they had guns instead of a big old whip. Never thought I'd be glad to see a bunch of guys with guns..."** Nate, just 11 years old, was found under a bed when police raided the drug house his mom and three big brothers ran.

"I get all that. **I got stuck with my four little brothers and sisters when mom left and didn't come back. I love them and everything, but being a mom to four kids under eight?** Seriously? By myself? They found mom last week down by the railroad tracks. Yeah, well, she's never coming home now. You know what I wish? **I wish Jesus could come down here and rebuild MY life in three days like He was going to fix His!!!"** BJ, the oldest in the group at 16, soon to be 17, was truly amazing simply for the fact that she survived her life – and kept her younger siblings safe – in one of the worst neighborhoods in the city.

We went on to talk about what kind of "temples" our lives were supposed to be, adding the following Scripture to our conversation: *"Or **do you not know that your body is a temple of the Holy Spirit** within you, which you have from God, and that you are not your own?"* (1 Corinthians 6:19, New Revised Standard Version)

Nate suddenly got excited (which rarely happened). "I got it!! **Jesus was telling them they needed to get a major remodel job.** You know, like they're doing at our Morris Cottage – that "renovation-thing", making it all new and stuff, yeah, like that."

That led to some life-changing and healing discussions over the next few weeks. We spent over a month just applying this Scripture to the healing process and future lives of these special young people.

These are the two questions that made all the difference:

How would Jesus "clean" the "Temple" of your life? What needs to be driven out? Not your family's, not anyone else's….but yours.

What needs to be rebuilt (renovated) in you so that you are whole and your life is indeed a "temple of the Holy Spirit"?

* * * * * * * * *

Jesus wasn't about destruction that day in the Temple. He was about renovation, about driving out everything that kept the Temple from being all that it was made to be. He drove out all that was about worldly profit in order to restore that which pointed to and glorified God.

Did you catch Jesus' words? "Destroy THIS Temple and…." You destroy this Temple, which you have made into a worldly-profit making enterprise, and **it will be rebuilt (for God-focused purpose and profit) in three days.** Hmmm.

Later the disciples would remember this scenario when Jesus was crucified and resurrected three days later. They thought they destroyed him when they crucified His human body, but three days later….holy renovation!! **Resurrected for heavenly purpose, He saves and directs us to eternal life with Him.**

* * * * * * * * *

Reflections…

Now it's your turn:

How would Jesus "clean" the "Temple" of your life? What needs to be driven out? Not your family's, not anyone else's….but yours.

What needs to be rebuilt (renovated) in you so that you are whole and your life is indeed a "temple of the Holy Spirit"?

10

Change the Channel!

*In Jerusalem during Passover many people put their faith in Jesus, because they saw Him work miracles. But Jesus knew what was in their hearts, and He would not let them have power over Him. **No one had to tell Him what people were like. He already knew.***

There was a man named Nicodemus who was a Pharisee and a Jewish leader. One night he went to Jesus and said, "Sir, we know that God has sent you to teach us. You could not work these miracles, unless God was with you."

Jesus replied, "I tell you for certain that you must be born from above before you can see God's kingdom."

*Nicodemus asked, "How can a grown man ever be born a second time?" Jesus answered, "I tell you for certain that before you can get into God's Kingdom, **you must be born not only by water, but by the Spirit.** Humans give life to their children. **Yet only God's Spirit can change you into a child of God.***

***Don't be surprised when I say that you must be born from above. Only God's Spirit gives new life.** The Spirit is like the wind that blows wherever it wants to. You can hear the wind, but you don't know where it comes from or where it is going."*
– John 2:23-3:8 (Contemporary English Version)

* * * * * * * * * *

I once had the blessing of meeting and praying with a young man who had just experienced a Kairos weekend, which is a Christian retreat held behind bars to bring incarcerated women and men into an active and deep relationship with Christ. In what I would call a "God-incidence", his weekend experience occurred just one week before his release from prison.

Introduced to me as "Nick", he quickly informed me that he was not named for "Saint Nicholas", but rather his full name was Nicodemus Paul. In fact, he very matter-of-factly said, **"It's OK to call me Nick though; it's better than some of the names guys called me in prison."**

Nick had come to the local coffee shop for a weekly men's reunion (sharing and prayer) group. We struck up a short conversation as we both waited for our drinks to come to the pickup window. He'd been out of prison just two weeks, but those two reunion group meetings had been vitally important to him. "Yep," he told me, **"These guys are walking with me as I change the channels of my life, just like my namesake Nicodemus did, right?"** Seeing my rather confused look (I wasn't making connections too quickly), he explained more.

"OK, the Book says that Jesus knew what people were like – for real, not what they wanted Him and everybody else to see – He knew what was in their heart, down in their gut. So He knew how they were tuned, what their focus was, how they made all their decisions, right?" I nodded. I was starting to get it – I thought.

"What Jesus was telling Nick in the Book was that he needed a new life. His focus was so messed up, it would get him in big trouble – eternal trouble – if he didn't get his whole life begun again. He needed to be reborn. Get it? I used to think that was a onetime thing, this holy channel-changing. I'm starting to get the fact that **it's really an everyday thing."**

Nick continued, "I've got the big channel-changing; that happened for me on my Kairos weekend. But now, my life needs to be refocused every day, tuned sharper and close to Him, to Jesus. **Now I have this little card on my bathroom mirror. Want to guess what it says?"** I guessed, "Change the Channel?" A big smile appeared on Nick's face. "You got it! Well. I see my new brothers coming in the door now. They're helping me, and I hope I'm helping them…change the channel!" With that, he turned to greet the guys in his reunion group.

* * * * * * * * *

Change the Channel. Nick was right. Jesus does indeed know our hearts. He knows how we really are. **Each day He invites us to trade our "old channels" for "new channels", to retune ourselves from worldly to holy focus. He opens new channels of grace in our lives each and every day.**

Nick experienced a whole weekend of "kairos". A "Kairos time" is one of change which we remember, one of life's bookmarks. Scripture has two words which refer to time: "chronos" refers to time measured by the clock; however, "kairos" refers to an event (or events) which change our lives, those which form the unique story of who we are and who we are becoming. Too often we spend all our focus on the "chronos" and ignore the "kairos" ways God is seeking to continually recreate us – our channel-changing times.

Reflections...

How do you intentionally change our life's "channels" so you too are born again each day to be deeper and closer disciples of our Lord and Savior?

I invite you to join me as I seek to be ever more open and eager to receive channel-changing kairos moments from God!

11

Saved…From What? For What?

*Nicodemus said to him, "**How can these things be?**" Jesus answered him, "Are you a teacher of Israel, and yet you do not understand these things? "Very truly, I tell you, we speak of what we know and testify to what we have seen; yet you do not receive our testimony. If I have told you about earthly things and you do not believe, how can you believe if I tell you about heavenly things? No one has ascended into heaven except the one who descended from heaven, the Son of Man.*

And just as Moses lifted up the serpent in the wilderness, so must the Son of Man be lifted up, that whoever believes in him may have eternal life. For God so loved the world that he gave his only Son, so that everyone who believes in him may not perish but may have eternal life.

*Indeed, **God did not send the Son into the world to condemn the world, but in order that the world might be saved through him.**"*   *-John 3:9-17, New Revised Standard Version*

*"**How are these things possible?**" Nicodemus asked. Jesus replied, "You are a respected Jewish teacher, and yet you don't understand these things? I assure you, we tell you what we know and have seen, and yet you won't believe our testimony. But if you don't believe me when I tell you about earthly things, how can you possibly believe if I tell you about heavenly things? No one has ever gone to heaven and returned. But the Son of Man has come down from heaven.*

And as Moses lifted up the bronze snake on a pole in the wilderness, so the Son of Man must be lifted up, so that everyone who believes in him will have eternal life. For God loved the world so much that he gave his one and only Son, so that everyone who believes in him will not perish but have eternal life.

*God **sent his Son into the world not to judge the world, but to save the world through him.**"*
                              -John 3:9-17, New Living Translation

*"**How can this be?**" Nicodemus asked. Jesus replied, "How can you be a teacher of Israel and not know these things? I tell you for certain we know what we are talking about because we have seen it ourselves. But none of you will accept what we say. If you don't believe when I talk to you about things on earth, how can you possibly believe if I talk to you about things in heaven? No one has gone up to heaven except the Son of Man, who came down from there."*

"And the Son of Man must be lifted up, just as the metal snake was lifted up by Moses in the desert. Then everyone who has faith in the Son of Man will have eternal life. God loved the people of this world so much that He gave His only Son, so that everyone who has faith in Him will have eternal life and never really die."

*"**God did not send His Son into the world to condemn its people. He sent Him to save them!**"*
                              -John 3:9-17, Contemporary English Version

*Nicodemus asked, **"What do you mean by this? How does this happen?"** Jesus said, "You're a respected teacher of Israel and you don't know these basics? Listen carefully. I'm speaking sober truth to you. I speak only of what I know by experience; I give witness only to what I have seen with my own eyes. There is no secondhand, no heresay. Yet instead of facing the evidence and accepting it, you procrastinate with questions. If I tell you things that are as plain as the hand before your face and you don't believe me, what use is there in telling you of things you can't see, the things of God?"*

*No one has ever gone up into the presence of God except the One who came down from that Presence, the Son of Man. In the same way that Moses lifted the serpent in the desert so people could have something to see and then believe, it is necessary for the Son of Man to be lifted up – and **everyone who looks up to Him, trusting and expectant, will gain a real life, eternal life.*** ·John 3:9-17, The Message Version*

* * * * * * * * *

"Guess what? I've been saved! I got saved in church last night!" The excited voice cut across at least four tables in the high school cafeteria, silencing pretty much every voice in its path. I looked over from my spot "on duty" by the doors a few yards away. My attention was drawn next to the line winding its way from the hallway past me into the cafeteria serving area.

Two young ladies had obviously witnessed the "saving proclamation". One I knew. Dora was one of the regular office helpers. Dora said to her friend, **"Wonder what he got saved from...somebody try to carjack him on the way to church or something?"** Her only answer a shrug, she continued. **"I mean, when you get saved <u>from</u> something, you're usually getting saved <u>for</u> something else...."**

A surprised look came over her friend's face. "Dora, you do realize he's talking about a church thing, a Jesus thing, right?" Since Dora still looked confused, her friend continued. **"I think it's in the Bible. Jesus, if you believe in Him, is supposed to 'save' you, to help you have a new, fresh life with a new focus—something like that."**

"OK", Dora looked like she was almost getting the idea. "So his life before last night is what he's saved <u>from</u>, right?" Her friend nodded, an encouraging expression on her face, as they inched forward in the cafeteria line. **"So what's going to be different <u>now</u>? And how can he start over again? What's he going to do with this exciting thing he calls 'getting saved'?"**

As the young ladies moved forward in line, I lost track of their conversation, but it made me think. Whatever it is we call that time when we accepted Jesus as Lord, the Leader of our lives, we are called to move from our old life-focus and priorities to new ones. We're called to identify, celebrate, and use the God-given gifts and talents for the sake of the Good News kingdom of Christ.

* * * * * * * * *

In John 3:6, Christ tells us that, *"...only God's Spirit can change you into a child of God."* We must accept this awesome Spirit-gift and put it to use as only we are created uniquely to do. Further, He says in John 3:17 (we like to stop at 3:16!) that, *"God did not send His Son into the world to condemn its people. He sent Him to save them!"* **We are thus saved <u>from</u> the results of our sin (condemnation) <u>for</u> a life filled with the Holy Spirit as we live and serve in the light of Christ.**

Dora's voice echoes that of Nicodemus as he asked Jesus, "How can a grown man be born a second time?" Incredible as it may seem, the eternal gift of Christ makes just that possible. **We are indeed saved by Christ <u>from</u> a worldly focus and set of priorities <u>to</u> a new life, reborn to an eternal, grace-filled focus in which we are called to live heavenly priorities.**

Reflections...

How does your life and the ways you use your uniquely God-created self show your own journey of being saved <u>from</u> the old focus, and <u>for</u>...eternal, grace-grounded living?

The young man who proclaimed his new life-focus on Christ that day in the cafeteria will soon find that this is an everyday, rest-of-his-life project. I pray that each day after that Sunday evening he is able to remind himself where he was, where he's headed, and Who (Jesus) his guide is!

May it also be so for each of us.

12

Holy Flashlights

Whoever believes in Him isn't judged; whoever doesn't believe in Him is already judged, because they don't believe in the name of God's only Son. This is the basis for judgment: **The light came into the world, and people loved darkness more than the light,** *for their actions are evil. All who do wicked things hate the light and don't come to the light for fear that their actions will be exposed to the light.*

Whoever does the truth comes to the light so that it can be seen that their actions were done in God."

- John 3:18-21, Common English Bible

Anyone who trusts in Him is acquitted; anyone who refuses to trust Him has long since been under the death sentence without knowing it. And why? Because of that person's failure to believe in the one-of-a-kind Son of God when introduced to Him. **This is the crisis we're in: God-light streamed into the world, but men and women everywhere ran for the darkness.** *They went for the darkness because they were not really interested in pleasing God. Everyone who makes a practice of doing evil, addicted to denial and illusion, hates God-light and won't come near it, fearing a painful exposure.*

But **anyone working and living in truth and reality welcomes God-light so the work can be seen for the God-work it is."**

- John 3:18-21, The Message Version

* * * * * * * * * *

After the Scripture above was read in worship, **it was "Children's Time", when young children came to the front of the sanctuary for a brief conversation about the text with one of the pastors.**

One child asked her question before even sitting down. **"Why would somebody choose to be in the dark? That's dumb!"** Before the pastor could respond, another youngster chimed in. "Yeah, that'd be real scary, like when me and my dad went camping last weekend. We made real sure to **take flashlights...and extra batteries too!"**

The pastor joined in the conversation. "So what do you think the Scripture we just read means?" Adele, an adorable six-year old, had an immediate response. "Well, duh! **We're supposed to be flashlights for Jesus, that's what it means."**

Responses came fast after that, a flood of words including:

"Like when I'm scared at night 'cause I hear monster noises, and my dad prays with me. He's a flashlight!"

"Or **when my friends want me to do something that looks fun** but it's really stupid, and I choose Jesus and presto! There's that flashlight!!"

"I get it! **Like when my grandma forgot who I was,** but she knew she loved me anyway. That had to be a Jesus flashlight in HER!"

After a minute or so of this, Pastor Amy noticed one child just quietly sitting, obviously deep in thought. **"Barry, what do you think?"** Quiet descended on the group, and all eyes turned to him. **At ten years old, Barry was one of the oldest** in the children's group. Next year he would move on to the junior youth group. Pastor Amy knew Barry as **a boy with extraordinary spiritual depth,** amazing in one so young.

"Well….," Barry began, obviously struggling for words. **"I think it's like when my little brother Stanley got cancer…and it took all of us to shine him home to Jesus.** It was all dark and scary but he never gave up. Before he went home he kept saying how Jesus was waiting for him. He told Mom that every time we prayed, he could see Jesus better. Now he's gone, but when everything seems all dark and sad I remember what he said. And **I choose Stanley's Jesus-flashlight. I want to see Jesus too."**

* * * * * * * * *

Why <u>would</u> someone choose darkness when they could have light? Sometimes we want to pretend that God can't see us making bad choices (and walking through the consequences). Funny thing, **when we make those "darkness" choices, they get easier and easier,** and as we get in the habit of choosing darkness over light, our lives grow darker and darker. The light gets harder and harder for us to see, let alone follow.

Young Barry could have chosen sadness (losing your five year old brother to brain cancer would do that for many of us), **but he followed the light of Christ** little Stanley shined for him. The whole family wrapped around Stanley as he went home to Jesus, "shining him home", as Barry expressed so well.

Young Elizabeth's grandmother, living with advancing Alzheimer's disease, didn't know Elizabeth's name, but she recognized the light in her. As she told a nurse one day after Elizabeth and her mom left, "I don't remember that little girl's name, but I just know she loves me, and I love her too." In the midst of the scary dark of dementia, even there - shining, and living in His light…

The light of Christ never ever goes away. He never gives up on us. He keeps sending light-bearers into our lives to "shine Jesus-flashlights" for us, pointing us back to a life of discipleship to Him. Once we choose the light (Christ-led choices based on our walk with Him as disciples), those choices get easier and easier too. We can move from walking in darkness to walking in His light!

* * * * * * * * *

Reflections...

Think of an area of your life that seems dark and perhaps even confusing to you. What choices could you make that would allow more of Christ's light to shine there?

Start by praying for that area. Then intentionally open your eyes and ears for the "flashlight-bearers" God will send into your life.

How have you made it through dark (sad, trying, confusing) times in your life?

How are you using those experiences to form you into a "flashlight-bearer" in someone else's life?

Start by praying for awareness and direction. You too can be a "flashlight-bearer" for Christ, lighting the path for others to a closer walk of discipleship with Him.

13

It's All About....Who?

Later, Jesus and His disciples went to Judea, where He stayed with them for a while and was baptizing people. John had not yet been put in jail. He was at Aenon near Salim, where there was a lot of water, and people were coming from there for John to baptize them.

John's followers got into an argument with a Jewish man about a ceremony of washing. They went to John and said, "Rabbi, you spoke about a man when you were with him east of the Jordan. He is now baptizing people, and everyone is going to him."

John replied, "No one can do anything unless God in heaven allows it. You surely remember how I told you that I am not the Messiah. I am only the one sent ahead of Him. At a wedding the groom is the one who gets married. The best man is glad just to be there and to hear the groom's voice. That's why I am so glad. Jesus becomes more important, while I become less important."
*   - John 3:22-30, Contemporary English Version*

After this conversation, Jesus went on with His disciples into the Judean countryside and relaxed with them there. He was also baptizing. At the same time, John was baptizing over at Aenon near Salim, where water was abundant. This was before John was thrown into jail.

John's disciples got into an argument with the establishment Jews over the nature of baptism. They came to John and said, "Rabbi, you know the one who was with you on the other side of the Jordan? The one you authorized with your witness? Well, now he's competing with us. He's baptizing too, and everyone's going to him instead of us."

John answered, "It's not possible for a person to succeed – I'm talking about eternal success – without heaven's help. You yourselves were there when I made it public that I was not the Messiah but simply the one sent ahead of Him to get things ready. The one who gets the bride is, by definition, the bridegroom. And the bridegroom's friend, his 'best man' – that's me – is in place at His side where He can hear every word, is genuinely happy. How could he be jealous when he knows that the wedding is finished and the marriage is off to a good start? That's why my cup is running over. This is the assigned moment for Him to move into the center, while I slip off to the sidelines."
*   -John 3:22-30, The Message Version*

* * * * * * * * *

His first hint should have been the collective response of fellow shoppers Saturday morning in the checkout line at the local hardware store. Exasperated after a long (and <u>finally</u> fruitful) search for a plumbing part, **Jared was venting his frustration** to anyone and everyone around him as he waited to check out.

An older guy behind him had a suggestion. **"Hey, I have a solution to your problem. They should just hire 'personal shopping assistants' - one for each shopper.** Yep, that'd do it. They'd line 'em up right inside the doors and they'd escort each shopper right to everything they needed."

Noting Jared's smile and nod, he continued. **"But then you know what that'd mean, right, son?"** *Jared hated being called 'son'...* "Well, son, that'd probably at least double their prices, wouldn't it? Hmmmm..." Jared fought the urge to roll his eyes. The man smiled as he delivered the punch line. "And then you and most of these other folks here would probably shop somewhere cheaper....someplace that wasn't....what do all those commercials say these days? **Oh yes, that 'all about you' malarkey. Why on earth people really believe all that, I've never figured out..."** Jared was SO glad when he finally reached the cashier, paid, and escaped that guy.

Later that day as he was driving his ten year old daughter to soccer practice, she (as usual) noticed the guy in the bizarre costume waving the big sign for the local payday loan place. **"Look Dad, look! Isn't he cool looking? When I grow up, I want a job like that.** Then all the people driving by will see me and wave. Wouldn't that be cool? Wow!!"

What? No way. **He could just see his Melanie in some weird costume waving a sign by the road.** What could make her want THAT job? "Honey, I know he looks cool, but it's not about him at all. It's really about what he's pointing to...you know, where he's trying to get people to go. And that's not such a great place."

Jared's daughter looked confused, so **he launched into a lecture about the evils of payday loan places.** After a few minutes, Jared realized that she wasn't paying any attention. So he asked, "What is it, honey?"

"Well, Daddy, like in the hardware store this morning? I love you Daddy, but, well, they were all looking at YOU. And...well...it wasn't very nice. Who was THAT about?"

Wow. Jared didn't even remember that Melanie had been with him. **He had been so wrapped up in needing it all to be about him.....** Now his own words came back to him. Where had he been pointing his young daughter to with his behavior in the store? Who <u>was</u> it all about?

Those thoughts (and regrets) were still swirling in his mind as he sat in church the next morning – so much so that **he missed the introduction of the guest speaker. But the speaker's first words hit him...hard...**

"I finally woke up," the speaker began, "It took over twenty years, but one day, BAM! It hit me. **My son was getting on my last nerve, and I found myself coming unglued. 'It's not about YOU!' That's what I yelled at him that day. And you know what he said? Here it is...ready? He asked me this: Well, who IS it about, Dad?"**

Tears filling the speaker's eyes, he continued. "I woke up that day. I thought it really <u>was</u> all about me. I mean that's what everybody trying to sell you something wants you to believe, right? And I sure did believe it."

Jared was paying attention now. He hadn't been to church in months, but something had made him come that day. Something...

The speaker continued, **"My name is Cary. I stand before you to confess that I couldn't for the life of me answer my son's question that day. Who WAS it all about?** I'd lost track way back in high school....maybe even middle school, I don't know. So there I was, a thirty-something year old husband and father of three, and I had no clue. And my kids were looking to ME to lead them, to point them to what life really WAS all about."

"You know, I think John faced the same temptation. He was quite the spectacle: wearing weird clothes and eating odd food, living in the desert….I'm sure lots of people thought it WAS about him. But no, **John was crystal clear. He wasn't the Messiah. John was not Jesus. And neither am I.** Like John, I'm a pointer. **My life is all about pointing the way,** inviting other people to join me following the One it really IS all about – Jesus."

"I'm supposed to become less and less important and He's supposed to become more and more important. After all, **none of <u>us</u> can give people eternal life, right?** After all – who are you going to follow to forever, to eternal life? Me? I don't think so! **"But – if I <u>point</u> you to <u>Him</u> – Ahhh, now we're going <u>somewhere</u>!"**

"So I ask you today: Who's it all about, really?"

✳ ✳ ✳ ✳ ✳ ✳ ✳ ✳ ✳

We all need to feel important. The question is, HOW important? John the Baptist was clear in his response to those who would make him the "main event". No. Wrong guy. John was important. He introduced people to Jesus; he announced Jesus; he continually pointed people to the real Savior, Messiah, Son of God.

We all need to be loved, respected, and cared for. But do we deserve greater amounts of love, care, and respect than others who are, like us, created in the image of God, precious in His sight? No.

Just like Jared, Cary, and John the Baptist, we are called to become less - so that the presence and invitation of Christ through us will become more and more. That's discipleship. It's about Jesus, the Christ.

✳ ✳ ✳ ✳ ✳ ✳ ✳ ✳ ✳

Reflections...

As you experienced Jared's story, what were your first thoughts?

If someone were to hang out with you for a day, who or what would your life point them to?

Reflections (continued)

As you grow and mature in discipleship to Christ, what are some changes you can make so your life more clearly demonstrates the joy and strength to be found when life really IS about following, and pointing others to, Christ?

14

The Baptism of Discipleship

The one who comes from above is above all; the one who is of the earth belongs to the earth and speaks about earthly things. The one who comes from heaven is above all. He testifies to what he has seen and heard, yet no one accepts his testimony.

Whoever has accepted his testimony has certified this, that God is true. *He whom God has sent speaks the words of God, for he gives the Spirit without measure. The Father loves the Son and has placed all things in his hands. Whoever believes in the Son has eternal life; whoever disobeys the Son will not see life, but must endure God's wrath.*

Now when Jesus learned that the Pharisees had heard, "Jesus is making and baptizing more disciples than John" -- although it was not Jesus himself but his disciples who baptized-- he left Judea and started back to Galilee.

- John 3:31 - 4:3, New Revised Standard Version

The one who comes from above is above all things. The one who is from the earth belongs to the earth and speaks as one from the earth. The one who comes from heaven is above all things. He testifies to what he has seen and heard, but no one accepts his testimony.

Whoever accepts his testimony confirms that God is true. *The One whom God sent speaks God's words because God gives the Spirit generously. The Father loves the Son and gives everything into His hands.* ***Whoever believes in the Son has eternal life.*** *Whoever doesn't believe in the Son won't see life, but the angry judgment of God remains on them.*

Jesus learned that the Pharisees had heard that He was making more disciples and baptizing more than John (although Jesus' disciples were baptizing, not Jesus Himself). Therefore, He left Judea and went back to Galilee.

- John 3:31 – 4:3, Common English Bible

* * * * * * * * *

After Easter worship came the much-awaited Easter egg hunt and games for the children (young and more experienced too), along with the delicious Easter potluck feast. What an exciting morning it had been! Nine had been baptized that morning, including seven youth. Soon the pastor and elders would give out baptismal certificates. As most of the people settled down at tables in the fellowship hall to eat and open Easter eggs (not necessarily in that order!), the sound system came on.

As each of those who had been baptized came forward to receive their baptismal certificates, they were invited to say a few words. Most simply said a quick "thank you", received their certificates and took their seats as the congregation applauded.

When Todd's name was called, he unfolded his 15 year old, six foot seven self from the folding chair and rose to his feet, looking through the assembled crowd.

Todd received his certificate, and the congregation clapped for him. The he stepped to the microphone. **"Probably not many of you know Gene and his wife Mary,"** he began, "but they've been coming to our Saturday church rummage sale for a long time. If you don't know these awesome people, you need to. **Gene doesn't know this, but he showed me Jesus one Saturday this year, right after I lost my grandpa.** You gotta know that my grandpa was tall like me. He understood how it felt to be called 'giant' and other, well, stuff I'm not gonna say here. So anyway, I was sitting on the curb outside taking a break from helping unload rummage stuff. **I was feeling pretty sorry for myself when Gene came over.** He just sat with me for a while. Didn't say anything till he got up to leave. Then he something I won't ever forget: **'You know, son, nobody's ever going to replace your grandpa, but God'll make sure you don't forget what he taught you – you just got to know that. You wanta talk ever, I'm here for ya.'** And he walked away."

Todd paused, composing himself as his voice began to crack.

Then he continued. "I didn't see Gene after that, until this morning. You know all of us youth picked out our baptismal robes last Sunday, and **I was SO glad to have the only one long enough for this body! Then I overheard Gene asking the pastor if he could get the 'baptism of discipleship' today...**"

Todd walked to a table in the back and invited an older couple seated there to join him. He helped Mary stand and then stood back as Gene, much like Todd (only much more slowly) unfolded his tall frame from the chair. When he straightened up, he stood eye to eye with Todd!

Quiet (unusual at these events) descended on the hall as they walked forward. **"Church, this is Gene, and his wife Mary. When he was a kid like me, they wouldn't baptize him because they didn't have any robes his size.** They told his mom she'd have to make him a robe, and they didn't have money for that, so he never got baptized. **Then the war came, and, well, he just gave up on church altogether.** So if you're wondering about my baptism-wet jeans, well, Gene's my – as he puts it - 'baptism of discipleship" buddy. He waited much longer than me to be baptized, so I gave him the robe."

Todd received his certificate, and Gene shared a hug with Todd as Todd returned to his seat. The pastor introduced Mary and Gene to the congregation. Mary's face glowed with happiness as Gene received his certificate and stepped to the microphone.

"Isn't Todd an amazing young man? In all my seventy-six years I've never met anyone like him. He's got Jesus all over him. And I'm telling you – when I stepped out of the water and looked into that deacon's eyes, I saw Jesus like I've never seen Him before. God showed me the truth in that moment – God baptized me into real discipleship – into a new life of REAL grace. Now I want Jesus to work through me like He worked through that deacon....and through young Todd, who gave me his baptism robe. **I want to be like them - the hands and feet, the voice, the heart....of Christ."**

* * * * * * * * *

Whoever has accepted his testimony has certified this, that God is true. *(Jn 3:33, NRSV)*

Whoever accepts his testimony confirms that God is true. *(Jn 3:33, CEB)*

This is a tall order! **Todd had lost his grandfather**, with whom he had lived since his parents were killed when he was five. **He lost the foundation of his life. Gene had lost hope in his life as he endured the realities of being a prisoner of war in World War II**. The foundations of his life were shaken in indescribable ways through that experience.

But one day at a church rummage sale God brought these two sons of His together, and new hope was born in each of them. One Easter morning these "baptism buddies" entered the waters of baptism and emerged with what Gene well-described as, "a new life of REAL grace."

That day, God became REAL and TRUE in a way they had never experienced before. How would they continue to experience that reality each day after that? That became the next challenge. Each day Todd and Gene would be challenged to confirm the gift received in Christ that Easter morning. **As Todd would later share with the youth group, he had experienced what he called the "Baptism of Discipleship", and his life was never <u>supposed</u> to be the same again!**

* * * * * * * * * *

Reflections...

If you have been baptized, what do you remember about that day? How is your life different because you to have received the "baptism of discipleship"?

If you were baptized when very young, what do you think your baptism meant to those who loved you? How is your life different because you to have received the "baptism of discipleship"?

If you haven't been baptized, what difference so you think baptism should make in someone's life?

Reflections (continued)

What does deciding to be baptized say about someone?

Many times, the life of intentional discipleship can be frustrating. We find ourselves nodding as we read, *"The one who comes from heaven is above all. He testifies to what he has seen and heard, yet no one accepts his testimony."* (Jn 3:32, NRSV)

Jesus promises to never leave us without His presence: *"And remember, I am with you always, to the end of the age."* (Mat 28:20b NRSV) Even when it seems our lives are caving in, when things will never be the same again, we can count on His presence to guide and strengthen us. It's the reality of accepting....the Baptism of Discipleship"!

15

Unfathomable Grace... from an Unlikely Guest

So he left Judea and returned to Galilee. He had to go through Samaria on the way. Eventually he came to the Samaritan village of Sychar, near the field that Jacob gave to his son Joseph. Jacob's well was there; and Jesus, tired from the long walk, sat wearily beside the well about noontime.

*Soon a Samaritan woman came to draw water, and Jesus said to her, "Please give me a drink." He was alone at the time because his disciples had gone into the village to buy some food. The woman was surprised, for Jews refuse to have anything to do with Samaritans. She said to Jesus, **"You are a Jew, and I am a Samaritan woman. Why are you asking me for a drink?"***

Jesus replied, "If you only knew the gift God has for you and who you are speaking to, you would ask me, and I would give you living water."

"But sir, you don't have a rope or a bucket," she said, "and this well is very deep. Where would you get this living water? And besides, do you think you're greater than our ancestor Jacob, who gave us this well? How can you offer better water than he and his sons and his animals enjoyed?"

*Jesus replied, "Anyone who drinks this water will soon become thirsty again. But **those who drink the water I give will never be thirsty again. It becomes a fresh, bubbling spring within them, giving them eternal life."***

"Please, sir," the woman said, "give me this water! Then I'll never be thirsty again, and I won't have to come here to get water."   *- John 4:3-15, New Living Translation*

So Jesus left the Judean countryside and went back to Galilee. To get there, He had to pass through Samaria. He came into Sychar, a Samaritan village that bordered the field Jacob had given his son Joseph. Jacob's well was still there. Jesus, worn out by the trip, sat down at the well. It was noon.

*A woman, a Samaritan, came to draw water. Jesus said, "Would you give me a drink of water?" (His disciples had gone into the village to buy food for lunch.) The Samaritan woman, taken aback, asked, **"How come you, a Jew, are asking me, a Samaritan woman, for a drink?"** (Jews in those days wouldn't be caught dead talking to Samaritans.)*

Jesus answered, "If you knew the generosity of God and who I am, you would be asking me for a drink, and I would give you fresh, living water."

The woman said, "Sir, you don't even have a bucket to draw with, and this well is deep. So how are you going to get this 'living water'? Are you a better man than our ancestor Jacob, who dug this well and drank from it, he and his sons and livestock, and passed it down to us?"

Jesus said, "Everyone who drinks this water will get thirsty again and again. Anyone who drinks the water I give will never thirst – not ever. The water I give will be an artesian spring within, gushing fountains of endless life."

The woman said, "Sir, give me this water so I won't ever get thirsty, won't ever have to come back to this well again!"   - *John 4:3-15, The Message Version*

* * * * * * * * * *

It hadn't seemed that far. With her car at the mechanic (how inconvenient that it broke down in the middle of a work week) Delores had decided to ride the bus. Who would have guessed that the morning bus routes could be so different from the evening routes? **Now a mile into the two-mile walk home from the bus stop, she wished she'd thought to bring extra water.** Five o'clock in Miami found the August temperatures still hovering above 100 degrees and Delores soaked in sweat. **Saving money by renting outside the not-so-great side of the city** meant a long walk through THAT part of town...

Life had been good that morning. Several folks had reached out of their cars to hand Felipe bottles of water as he stood in the middle of the busy intersection trying to sell the rest of his allotted newspapers. To **Felipe, a newly arrived refugee**, the advertisement promising "up to a thousand dollars a week" was turning out to be a fantasy. **He had hoped to move his family out of the homeless shelter months ago, but...**at least his three children were loving school and they had food to eat.

Delores kept walking. Up ahead she could see a homeless guy selling newspapers. He looked friendly. Maybe he had some water to spare, even a swallow or two...

Felipe spotted her as she approached. As she came closer, he noticed the weariness in her walk. Then he saw her face, dripping with sweat. **He wanted to help, but who was he?** Just some homeless guy they all thought was "one of those Mexicans". He'd been scowled at, spit on, and worse. But this lady looked like she'd fall down any minute. But she looked too fancy for the likes of him. Felipe had learned a lot in his six months here.....but still...

Now that she could see him up close, the newspaper guy looked OK.... "Excuse me, sir...?" A shocked face looked up at her.

Sir? This lady called him Sir! Felipe looked up...into the startlingly green eyes of Delores. "Sir, would you by any chance have....I mean...**could I have a couple swallows of your water?**" She didn't quite know how to interpret the shocked look on Felipe's face. Did she look that bad? Was she scaring him?

"Y..you want a drink from ME?" She nodded. "Of course. Of course I will share with you." He couldn't believe it – this woman was looking him in the eye. Nobody here ever did that...well, almost never. And then she held out her hand!

"Hi, I'm Delores. And you surely are heaven-sent today!" Felipe wiped his hand on his jeans and reached out to shake her hand. As he opened his backpack and gave her a bottle of water, she smiled. She looked him in the eye....and smiled!

"Well...Delores...haven't seen much heaven around this place yet. It's sure not what I imagined it would be, not at all. I could use a little, as you call it, 'heaven-sent'!" Felipe stepped away a moment to sell a couple of papers. Delores looked around. "I know you're busy, but thanks so much for the drink, Felipe." Delores began to walk away, and then she had an idea. **"What if there was a place you could sell all those papers that was safe and had plenty of water to drink?"**

Felipe laughed. *Was she serious?* "Well, **I would truly call that, as you say, 'heaven-sent'!"**

Delores smiled as the idea took shape in her mind. **"And what if…what if your wife could have a job there part time too?"**

Now Felipe KNEW he was dreaming! His wife, her English wasn't so good yet, but she was learning. She'd been trying to find a job ever since they got here.

"Yes Felipe, I manage a small coffee shop in that office building down the street there, and I need someone to clean tables and welcome busy people to relax with a cup of coffee…and a paper of course!"

Felipe sat down on his stack of papers, traffic around him forgotten for the moment. But Delores wasn't finished. **"I have another idea too, Felipe. The apartment I have, well, I have extra room.** It has three bedrooms, I'm only really using one. How about this: You come and be my newspaper seller and I'll pay you by sharing my place with you and your family?"

WHAT? What a drink from heaven this was! A place to live. A job for Maria. No more homeless shelter. This was amazing, a true gift from heaven! **"W…why are you doing this?"** Felipe just had to ask.

Delores took a breath. **"OK, here's the truth: You gave me a wonderful, but temporary drink. I want to share with you the forever drink someone gave me when I was struggling too – I want to share the amazing gift of Christ.** Because you see, we think we know what we need, but He KNOWS what we need. **We need heaven-sent, forever, never-running-out water. Somebody shared it with me, and now I want to share it with you.** Will you share it with me?"

And that was the beginning of a grace-filled, amazing relationship.

* * * * * * * * *

Who was the guest? Was it a struggling, overheated Delores, who was offered a drink? Or Felipe, who was offered work and shelter?

Who was the host? Was it Delores, who offered to share her home and offered Felipe and Maria better jobs? Or Felipe who offered her a drink from his meager supply?

The truth is, Jesus was the host. Both Felipe and Delores were His guests. And truly, Jesus was their guest as they shared heaven-sent grace with one another. He was their guest too. Both received unfathomable grace…. from an unlikely guest. Neither would have predicted the events of this day. **And their lives would never be the same.**

This unfathomable grace is offered to us on a regular basis. We encounter the presence of Christ in one another daily. **We are such unlikely guests!** But not only does Christ persistently extend the invitation to us as His guests of grace, He invites us to extend that same invitation to one another – to see His face, to hear His voice – in each other.

As His disciples, we are to welcome others to His banquet of…unfathomable grace!

* * * * * * * * *

Reflections...

Did you identify with Felipe more...or Delores? Or perhaps neither? Why do you think this is?

In what ways has God's grace been a surprise in your life?

How are you, like Felipe, sharing what you have, knowing God will multiply it in that sharing in amazing ways?

How are you, like Delores, looking beyond worldly judgments of those you meet to find the grace and presence of Christ in them?

Remember: *"Anyone who drinks the water I give will never thirst – not ever. The water I give will be an artesian spring within, gushing fountains of endless life."*

16

Could He Be... for ME?

The woman said to him, "Sir, give me this water, so that I may never be thirsty or have to keep coming here to draw water." Jesus said to her, "Go, call your husband, and come back."

The woman answered him, "I have no husband." Jesus said to her, "You are right in saying, 'I have no husband'; for you have had five husbands, and the one you have now is not your husband. What you have said is true!"

The woman said to him, "Sir, I see that you are a prophet. Our ancestors worshiped on this mountain, but you say that the place where people must worship is in Jerusalem."

*Jesus said to her, "Woman, believe me, the hour is coming when you will worship the Father neither on this mountain nor in Jerusalem. You worship what you do not know; we worship what we know, for salvation is from the Jews. **But the hour is coming, and is now here, when the true worshipers will worship the Father in spirit and truth, for the Father seeks such as these to worship him. God is Spirit, and those who worship him must worship in spirit and truth.**"*

The woman said to him, "I know that Messiah is coming" (who is called Christ). "When he comes, he will proclaim all things to us." Jesus said to her, "I am he, the one who is speaking to you."

Just then his disciples came. They were astonished that he was speaking with a woman, but no one said, "What do you want?" or, "Why are you speaking with her?"

Then the woman left her water jar and went back to the city. She said to the people, "Come and see a man who told me everything I have ever done! He cannot be the Messiah, can he?" They left the city and were on their way to him.

- John 4:15-30, New Revised Standard Version

The woman said, "Sir, give me this water so I won't ever get thirsty, won't ever have to come back to this well again!"

He said, "Go call your husband and then come back." "I have no husband," she said.

"That's nicely put: 'I have no husband.' You've had five husbands, and the man you're living with now isn't even your husband. You spoke the truth there, sure enough."

"Oh, so you're a prophet! Well, tell me this: Our ancestors worshiped God at this mountain, but you Jews insist that Jerusalem is the only place for worship, right?"

*"Believe me, woman, the time is coming when you Samaritans will worship the Father neither here at this mountain nor there in Jerusalem. You worship guessing in the dark; we Jews worship in the clear light of day. God's way of salvation is made available through the Jews. **But the time is coming – it has, in fact, come – when what you're called will not matter and where you go to worship will not matter. It's who you are and the way you live that count before God. Your worship must engage your spirit in the pursuit of truth. That's the kind of people the***

Father is out looking for: those who are simply and honestly themselves before Him in their worship. God is sheer being itself – Spirit. Those who worship Him must do it out of their very being, their spirits, their true selves, in adoration."

The woman said, "I don't know about that. I do know that the Messiah is coming. When He arrives, we'll get the whole story." "I am He," said Jesus. "You don't have to wait any longer or look any further."

Just then His disciples came back. They were shocked. They couldn't believe He was talking with that kind of woman. No one said what they were all thinking, but their faces showed it.

The woman took the hint and left. In her confusion she left her water pot. Back in the village she told the people, "Come see a man who knew all about the things I did, who knows me inside and out. Do you think this could be the Messiah?" And they went out to see for themselves.   *- John 4:3-15, The Message Version*

* * * * * * * * * *

As the young adult music team arrived and began unloading instruments and equipment for the new contemporary worship service, the **drummer noticed someone hanging around the church's new outdoor prayer and meditation area.**

"Hey Brian, look. There she is again. She was there on the bench last week, wasn't she?" Em wondered what the woman's story was. She'd noticed her sitting on the bench under the old oak tree the last few Sundays when they'd come to get everything set up and practice before worship.

Brian shrugged as they went into the church together. **"Probably one of those homeless people that hang around hoping for food or booze or something.** And if we let her in, then more of her kind will come, and then, who knows? I just hope she leaves soon so she doesn't chase any new people away."

Terry motioned them inside as he juggled the door along with his music stand and guitar. "You know, **as far as that 'chasing thing', she looks pretty old, I mean, how fast do you think she could move?** Really, chasing people? Seriously?"

Brian noticed the thoughtful look on Terry's face. "No, buddy. Don't do it. **Leave her alone. Who knows where she's been?"** Clearly exasperated, Brian headed into the church to set up.

Terry's expression changed in an instant - from thoughtful to determined as he turned around and went back out the door. "You guys go ahead and set up. My instrument travels light; self contained, you might say." (Terry was the lead singer.) As he crossed the church lawn toward the meditation area and the woman sitting on the bench, **his breath caught in his throat.** This woman could have been his grandmother's sister!

She looked up as Terry approached, gathering her bag and clearly expecting him to tell her to leave. But she hesitated as he smiled at her. **"Morning, m'am. How are you today? It's a little chilly out here, isn't it?** Want to come inside and get warm for a bit? The music we're playing might not be quite what you've heard in church before, but…." *Why do I run on at the mouth so much when I get nervous?* Terry made himself stop talking.

"No, that's OK, really. I'll just pray on this bench out here. **You <u>really</u> don't want me in your church. It's been so long since I've been in a church,** don't know as I'd recognize too much of the music anyway. But,… well,…. if you could say a little prayer for me…that'd be real nice." As she spoke, **Terry couldn't shake the feeling that he knew this lady.** He reached in his wallet and pulled out an old picture.

"Oh, I love pictures," she said as she tried to see, "Can I look?" Terry looked from the picture to the woman's face and back again. "This is weird….you look so much like…" She smiled as she reached in her bag. "By the way, my name's May, like the month of May. Perhaps you recognize this picture?" **May pulled out an old yellowed photo of two little boys and their grandparents.**

"How….when….where did you get this?" Terry couldn't believe it. He was looking at a picture of himself, his little brother, and their grandparents. "Terrence, right? Well, Terrence, it's like this. I was the 'bad girl' in the family." She pointed at Terry's grandmother. "She was my sister Patricia. We called her Patty. Heard she passed not too long ago. Sorry to hear that, real sorry." Terry's mind was still spinning. *Was this the Aunt May everybody said died a long time ago?*

"Confusing, isn't it? Well, no, I didn't die, just died to the family I guess. Made a lot of bad choices I did, a lot, so I guess they just killed me off, in their minds anyway. But I figure you're old enough, and I've changed enough, that I wanted to know who you'd become. So I came looking."

Stunned (almost) speechless, Terry started to stand up as he noticed Em peeking out the church doors to see where he'd gone. "Come on in and listen to us play. You're welcome, really." May smiled. "Nope, probably not. See, a long time ago, when I finally got pregnant, that was the last straw. **My folks threw me out, and the church threw me out too. I've never been back to either one.** Besides, my life's been so messed up for so long, **I don't figure Jesus wants the likes of me anyway."**

Terry looked up to see Brian striding purposefully across the grass. *Uh oh, here it comes.* "Hey, Brian, I want you to meet my long lost Aunt May." Brian ignored May and pointed a finger at Terry. "You need to get in here. We need to get ready. See, people are starting to pull into the lot."

"Just a minute, May….Aunt May….don't go away...please." Terry walked a few steps away with Brian, who was getting more impatient by the second. Brian pointed that finger at him again. **"OK, Terry, enough. If we invite her, pretty soon all her friends will come too, and we'll have homeless people camped out all over, and….."**

Terry bristled with anger. "So…? **Isn't it about time *somebody* invited her to know Jesus?** Isn't Jesus for her too? Or is He only for some people, maybe 'acceptable' people?" With that, he walked back to the bench, helped May up, and brought her into the church.

She hesitated at the doors. "Won't they be shocked, I mean really, **would Jesus want me in here?** Me?"

Now even more sure of his decision, Terry answered. "Yes, Jesus IS for you. He's ALWAYS been for you. **It's people who've been the problem, not Jesus.** He is specifically, completely, eternally for you. And don't you listen ever again to anyone who tells you anything different."

* * * * * * * * *

True story? Yes. Did more of "those people" come? Again, yes indeed. You see, Terry's long-lost (but now completely found) Aunt May was a 71-year-old homeless woman living in a wooded campsite with a group of her friends. She returned 'home' to them that day and invited them to come meet her long-lost great nephew.

Soon, the contemporary service had three rows of May's friends (and their friends). You see, **like the "woman at the well" whom Jesus met that noonday, May went back and told her friends** that Jesus would welcome them too. Jesus was for her, and for them, too!

Did everyone accept those whom May invited to worship? Sadly, no. Brian left the worship team and joined another church, one where he figured "those people" wouldn't be so welcome. Em struggled about whether she should stay, but ultimately she stayed as the worship service grew….and grew. They discovered one of May's friends was a very talented guitarist, and he joined the worship team.

And that worship service got a new name. It became known as the "Yes, Jesus welcomes YOU" service. The welcome was big. The welcome was broad. And the welcome was deep. Lives were changed as Christ lived, and moved, and breathed the Spirit among them!

* * * * * * * * *

Reflections…

Have you ever met someone who was ostracized (rejected, shunned, kicked out) of their family and/or church? What were/are your thoughts?

Have you had such an experience yourself? If so, how did others react? How do you think Jesus would teach them to respond?

Many times, we are conditioned not to even notice people "on the margins" of life. Jesus spent much of His life and ministry in two contrasting worlds – among the learned (Pharisees, Sadducees, Jewish leaders) – and among the outcast (lepers, tax collectors, and various kinds of 'sinners', including the 'woman at the well').

How can we learn from Him to include all kinds of people in our lives?

17

Grandpa's Peaches

Meanwhile the disciples were urging him, "Rabbi, eat something." But he said to them, **"I have food to eat that you do not know about."**

So the disciples said to one another, "Surely no one has brought him something to eat?"

Jesus said to them, **"My food is to do the will of him who sent me and to complete his work.** *Do you not say, 'Four months more, then comes the harvest'? But I tell you, look around you, and see how the fields are ripe for harvesting. The reaper is already receiving wages and is gathering fruit for eternal life, so that sower and reaper may rejoice together. For here the saying holds true,* **'One sows and another reaps.'** *I sent you to reap that for which you did not labor. Others have labored, and you have entered into their labor."*   *- John 4:31-38, New Revised Standard Version*

While this was happening, Jesus' disciples were saying to Him, "Teacher, please eat something." But Jesus told them, **"I have food you don't know anything about."**

His disciples started asking each other, "Has someone brought Him something to eat?"

Jesus said, **"My food is to do what God wants!** *He is the one who sent me, and I must finish the work that He gave me to do. You may say there are still four months until harvest time. But I tell you to look, and you will see that the fields are ripe and ready to harvest. Even now the harvest workers are receiving their reward by gathering a harvest that brings eternal life. Then everyone who planted the seed and everyone who harvests the crop will celebrate together. So the saying proves true,* **'Some plant the seed, and others harvest the crop.'** *I am sending you to harvest crops in fields where others have done all the hard work."*   *- John 4:31-38, Contemporary English Version*

* * * * * * * * * *

Picking peaches was hard work! As Amos hauled yet another bushel basket of peaches up the back porch steps, he looked up into the smiling face of his grandma Hattie. **"How many more peaches do you need, Grandma?"**

Hattie heard the distinct sound of whining in young Amos's voice. **"God put a lot of work into growing all those peaches, Amos. Who are we to waste God's hard work?** There's only one more row of trees to pick. Gotta pick 'em before you can eat 'em, right? And I know you love my peach jam!"

Well…OK, grandma Hattie had a point there. She made the best peach jam (and peach cobbler, and peach pie, and…..) that he'd ever tasted. People came from miles around to buy it at the local farmer's market, and the orders had already started coming for all of it. Amos carried the latest bushel into the big kitchen, put it down next to the growing row of baskets full of peaches, and headed out the door again, picking up an empty basket from the back porch as he went.

Hattie smiled out the kitchen window. Amos sure was growing up fast! She wiped a tear from the corner of her eye as she watched him walk out to the orchard. **When he turned a certain way.....Amos was the spitting image of her sweet Anthony, Hattie's husband of forty-three years.** She'd lost him to cancer two long years ago today. Some days, it seemed like yesterday he was right beside her in the kitchen, bringing in the very first peaches from their brand new ten-tree orchard. And then there were days like today, when she missed him so much and it seemed like he'd been gone forever.

Lost in thoughtful memories, Hattie suddenly realized Amos was coming with another bushel of peaches. My, how time flew! The orchard's fifty peach trees were a beautiful sight. **Last year on this day, Hattie had planted five trees in memory of her sweetheart, and today they would plant five more.**

"You're doing such a wonderful job, Amos! I've got turkey sandwich, chips, and peaches for lunch. Come sit down and eat; we'll need the energy for this afternoon. *Oh no. What else could grandma have planned?* Amos was hoping to get away to shoot some hoops with friends at the local park after lunch. **"So, grandma, what's up for this afternoon?"**

Grandma Hattie smiled. **"Well, today's grandpa's Heaven-Day anniversary. We're planting his five trees;** they're waiting for us around the side of the house in the shade. One of these days, we'll have those hundred trees he dreamed of!"

Later that afternoon, Amos and Grandma Hattie sat on the porch drinking tall glasses of her best-in-the-world lemonade. Grandma got that serious look she always had right before she said something really important, so he put his glass down to listen.

"Amos, I have something important to tell you. **You're sixteen now, and I think you need to know."** Now Amos sat up even straighter. "OK, grandma. Are you OK?"

"Well.....Amos, I will be...OK, that is. It's time for you to know that your grandpa Anthony and I, well, we love you so much, and from the time you were a tiny guy you've been such a help to us, coming to stay with us every summer...every single summer, even when I know we're not the most exciting company for a growing-up young man."

Amos didn't like the way this talk was going. "Are you OK, grandma?" She hesitated. Amos worried more.

"Like I said, I will be. **What I need to tell you is that we're leaving this place to you when my Heaven-Day comes.** You need a place of your own, and you've earned it." As she took a breath to continue, Amos couldn't help himself. He interrupted (again).

"Seriously? You know my dream is to be a farmer. Seriously? You've got over a hundred acres here. Don't you need it? I mean, you could sell it and travel like you've always talked about, and....seriously, Grandma?"

"Well, Amos, that's the other thing I need to tell you. **Where I'll be traveling soon, I won't need any of this.** Grandpa and I, we started the hundred-tree orchard dream, and you're the one to make it grow. You know what they say, some plant, some water, and some harvest, and all those "somes" aren't necessarily the same. You are an amazing young man, Amos, and I know God has great plans for you, I'm sure of it!"

Amos didn't hear much past Grandma's "Where I'll be traveling soon..." sentence. He took another breath, this time waiting so he wouldn't interrupt her. "Where are you going, Grandma?"

"Why, Amos, my Heaven-Day is coming, that's what. Haven't been feeling so lively, so I went to check it out. It's cancer, same as what sent your grandpa Anthony to be with the Lord. **They think my Heaven-Day will be here pretty soon, in fact.**"

Amos felt the tears sting his eyes. *What? Grandma Hattie was his favorite person in the whole world. She'd been there through everything...his mom leaving, his truck-driver dad struggling to raise four boys while making a living. Grandpa Anthony had been his rock, but Grandma....Grandma Hattie was his heart. What would he do without her?*

"I can guess what you're thinking. **Here's what you'll do, Amos. You will plant, and you will harvest. Then one day other folks will harvest what you planted, and they'll plant, and on it goes.** Always remember that God works hardest of all. He put all this here, and it's our job to take care of it."

* * * * * * * * *

I like Grandma's concept of "Heaven-Day". What if we all lived like dying to this world was indeed a celebration of our Heaven-Day? How would we plant God's seeds, water and nourish those planted by those before us, and enjoy the heaven-sent harvest?

Amos shared the story above at his Grandma Hattie's memorial service. He went on to plant ten more peach trees every year, five on grandpa Anthony's Heaven-Day and five on Grandma Hattie's. When he reached a hundred peach trees, he began a cherry tree orchard. He married Dorothy (Dot to her friends), and together they picked peaches and cherries, made jams, pies, and cobblers, and had amazing fun selling them at local farmers markets. Dot added a big vegetable garden. When their daughter Harriet (they called her Hattie) was old enough, they told her the story of "Grandpa's peaches". They laughed, tears in their eyes as they watched little Hattie pick peaches with her little five-year-old fingers, listening to her giggle with glee as she added them to the baskets in the orchard.

* * * * * * * * *

Reflections...

The "heavenly food" Jesus teaches His disciples about is that which continues growing as generation after generation of us celebrate our "Heaven-Days". Note that Jesus told them that this was food they "don't know anything about". The food He taught them about, the eternal, lasts-forever kind, is "to do the will of Him who sent Me," or in other words, "to do what God wants."

How would you describe this kind of food?

Reflections (continued)

We spend much of our time and attention on growing what we want. Our focus is drawn to the temporary; we have the illusion we can control the planting, watering, and harvesting. We are so tempted to plant and grow for our own gain, our own harvest. God's creation, and God's care, know no favorite generation of people. God's seeds are not our seeds; but He <u>has</u> given us care and stewardship of them.

What about those who come after us – in what ways can we help plant God's seeds?

Where in your life are you being called to water and grow the kind of seeds Jesus is teaching about in this Scripture?

What have you harvested that others have planted (begun) and grown?

When your Heaven-Day arrives, may you too be in the celebration where, *"…everyone who planted the seed and everyone who harvests the crop will celebrate together."*!

18

Who Says?

Many Samaritans from that city believed in him because of the woman's testimony, "He told me everything I have ever done." *So when the Samaritans came to him, they asked him to stay with them; and he stayed there two days. And many more believed because of his word.*

They said to the woman, **"It is no longer because of what you said that we believe, for we have heard for ourselves, and we know that this is truly the Savior of the world."**

When the two days were over, he went from that place to Galilee (for Jesus himself had testified that a prophet has no honor in the prophet's own country). When he came to Galilee, the **Galileans welcomed him, since they had seen all that he had done in Jerusalem at the festival;** *for they too had gone to the festival.*

- John 4:39-45, New Revised Standard Version

Many Samaritans in that city believed in Jesus because of the woman's word when she testified, "He told me everything I've ever done." *So when the Samaritans came to Jesus, they asked Him to stay with them, and He stayed there two days. Many more believed because of His word, and they said to the woman,* **"We no longer believe because what you said, for we have heard for ourselves and know that this one is truly the Savior of the world."**

After two days, Jesus left for Galilee. (Jesus Himself had testified that prophets have no honor in their own country.) When He came to Galilee, the **Galileans welcomed Him because they had seen all the things He had done in Jerusalem during the festival,** *for they also had been at the festival.*   *- John 4:39-45, Common English Bible*

* * * * * * * * *

Marissa was SO done with all her parents' old fogie advice and restrictions. What could possibly be wrong with getting a little tattoo? I mean, it wasn't like she wanted to get "satan-lover" or some bizarre thing tattooed on her forehead! And she and Brad (love of her life) had decided to get each others' names (in gorgeous script) tattooed on their arms. Maybe some flowers or hearts or something too....

"Ahhhh....no." **Why did Marissa's parents have to be so stubborn?** And then there was the nose stud Brad had helped her pick out – beautiful amethyst in a gold stud. Just a little nose pierce...what was their big deal? **Who says** it's such a bad idea?

"Aren't you looking for a job? Tats and piercings won't help you with that." That was dad's favorite line any time the tattoo/piercing topic came up. And the looks...mom was an expert at 'the look' when she was disappointed. She found herself muttering an irritated **"Who says?"** under her breath.

Marissa stopped in the hall after her last class as she heard her best friend Valerie call her name. "Hey 'Rissa, stop!" Val hoisted her backpack over her shoulder. **"Want to go apply at the new store that's opening up? They put a 'hiring' sign out this morning, and cars are in the lot!"**

"Well, I kind of had plans with Brad. He wants to go get our tats today. Cool, huh?" Marissa looked at Val, expecting shared excitement. "'Rissa, wait. **You know you'll have to cover tats at work, right?** And lots of places won't like the nose stud either, and you've got to wear a stud for quite a while after it's done, or it'll close up again. And, well...I really didn't want to tell you this, but you know that new girl in Chem class? Well, Brad asked to move to her lab group, and he's been walking her all over the place too. How serious are you two? You really want to have his name...tattooed...on your arm? **Who says** that's a good idea? That's pretty permanent..."

Marissa stopped in the middle of the busy hallway. "Wow, Val, you serious? So you have to wear long sleeves, or what?" Val stopped beside her. "Well, that or cover them up with ace bandages. Uuugly!"

Their conversation continued as they walked to the school parking lot together. After an afternoon of studying at the library, Marissa arrived at home just as mom and dad were setting the table for dinner. **"Hey, Mom.. Dad, I've decided not to get that tattoo after all.** Maybe when I'm older like you, and I already have a job and everything, but not now. And if I got my nose pierced right now, and I couldn't wear a stud at work, the hole would just close up and it would be a waste of money, right?"

Both mom and dad froze in their tracks, happy, relieved, but truly stunned. **What happened?**

* * * * * * * * *

What happened indeed? The difference for Marissa happened when her friend, her peer, testified to her about the probable consequences of the choices Marissa was about to make. No matter what her parents (old, after all....what would they understand?) advised, when Val spoke, Marissa listened. **Who said? Val did. Marissa believed. She acted.**

And then? Then she experienced the job search. Time after time, she learned that she would indeed have to cover any tattoos to get (and keep) most of the retail and food service jobs she was applying for. Several times she noticed interviewers looking closely at her face and wondered. In three of the interviews she had, they let her know the only piercings allowed, "adornments" as they put it, were ears. She was so glad she'd listened to Val....and her parents too.

The truth is, **the more we have in common with someone, the more closely we listen to and value what they say to us.** It matters. We act on it. Scripture tells us many of those to whom this Samaritan woman testified upon her return for meeting Jesus "believed". Many more were attracted to go and see what she was talking about. And they probably told others, who told others, who....

* * * * * * * * *

Reflections...

"Who says?" It really does matter. Who do you listen to the most closely? Why do you value their words more than those of others in your life?

Take a moment to think: All of us have at least one person in our lives who highly value our opinions and advice. Who is that in your life?

Following the example of this Samaritan woman, how do your words and actions testify that Jesus is part of your life?

A common saying is: "Be a friend. Make a friend. Draw your friend to Christ." Take another moment to think (and perhaps plan). Who is God placing in your life right now for whom you could do this? When will you begin?

19

Prove It!

Then he came again to Cana in Galilee where he had changed the water into wine. Now there was a royal official whose son lay ill in Capernaum. When he heard that Jesus had come from Judea to Galilee, he went and begged him to come down and heal his son, for he was at the point of death.

*Then Jesus said to him, **"Unless you see signs and wonders you will not believe."** The official said to him, "Sir, come down before my little boy dies."*

Jesus said to him, "Go; your son will live." The man believed the word that Jesus spoke to him and started on his way.

As he was going down, his slaves met him and told him that his child was alive. So he asked them the hour when he began to recover, and they said to him, "Yesterday at one in the afternoon the fever left him."

The father realized that this was the hour when Jesus had said to him, "Your son will live." So he himself believed, along with his whole household. Now this was the second sign that Jesus did after coming from Judea to Galilee.

- John 4:46-54, New Revised Standard Version

While Jesus was in Galilee, He returned to the village of Cana, where He had turned the water into wine. There was an official in Capernaum whose son was sick. And when the man heard that Jesus had come from Judea, he went and begged Him to keep his son from dying.

*Jesus told the official, **"You won't have faith unless you see miracles and wonders!"** The man replied, "Lord, please come before my son dies!"*

Jesus then said, "Your son will live. Go on home to him." The man believed Jesus and started back home. Some of the official's servants met him along the road and told him, "Your son is better!" He asked them when the boy got better, and they answered, "The fever left him yesterday at one o'clock."

The boy's father realized that at one o'clock the day before, Jesus has told him, "Your son will live!" So the man and everyone in his family put their faith in Jesus. This was the second miracle that Jesus worked after He left Judea and went to Galilee.

- John 4:46-54, The Message Version

✶ ✶ ✶ ✶ ✶ ✶ ✶ ✶ ✶ ✶

"I tried that 'Jesus thing', and nothing happened!" The exasperated young man sat on the end of his cot in the rehab house. This place wasn't fixing anything in his life. The truth was, he'd checked in here because the judge told him it was either here or the county jail.

He didn't realize anyone heard him until an answer came from the doorway.

"Well, may I ask what you expected to happen?" Some old guy stepped into Blake's room…well, the room he shared with three other guys, that is.

"Huh? What do you mean, 'what did I expect?' **This IS one of those 'Jesus places', right?"**

The man nodded. "Uh huh, I'm pretty sure it is."

"Well then, coming here's supposed to make me all better then, right? I mean, that's what I'm hearing all over the place. 'Jesus saves.' 'Jesus heals.' All that…..stuff. **Well, when's my turn?** That's what I want to know."

"Name's Gene, and I meant what I said. What do you expect? I mean, are you looking for lightning bolts from heaven, or…what?"

"Well, I guess I was waiting for the proof. I expected to not crave the drugs. I expected them to get me a job. I expected to not be stuck in this place too long."

"Wow, Blake, is it? Well, Blake, seems like what you expect is some kind of show! I mean, if Jesus was to swoop down here and wave His hands over you, hand you a job, and give you keys to your brand new apartment, would that do it?"

Now Blake sat up, excited. "Oh yeah, yes it would! So when will THAT happen?"

Gene shook his head sadly. **"Son, I think you must have a fever.** You know there's a guy Jesus talked with once kinda like you. Let me see….yep, Jesus met him on a road, and he wanted to see some showy miracles too. Want to know what Jesus did do? No matter, gonna tell you anyway. **Jesus did not fix all this guy's problems. Did not make the guy's son a perfect boy. Nope. All Jesus did was…ready? All He did was cure the boy's fever. That's it. The rest was up to him."**

Blake looked up at Gene. "So how long you been working here? Bet you've seen a lot, huh?"

Gene smiled. "Well, the truth is, my son's the one who works here. He runs the front desk. Me, well, he's been letting me 'hang out', he calls it. Not too sure what that means. **Maybe I'm kinda like you in a way."**

"No way, old man. You don't have the look, I mean…." Blake was really curious now.

"No, listen. I get what that 'fix me, Jesus' prayer feels like. You lost your mind on drugs, right? But you're getting it back, I can tell. One step at a time. **Me, I'm losing my mind one step at a time. They call it Alzheimer's; I call it hell.** Yesterday I forgot to tie my shoes and about broke my neck, that's what I did. But my son was right. Here, I can start again. This old Korean War soldier can begin again. **I found a purpose here today. Jesus took care of my fever too – my 'everything's gotta be perfect' fever.** I welcome people here. I listen. I care. That's my 'post-fever' life. What's yours gonna be? You get to decide…and you get to get with it and work for it. What do you say?"

"Wow. Truth is, I think there may be something to this 'Jesus-stuff'. Know what I was getting ready to do before you walked in here? I was going to leave. Just walk right out. I said one last, plain prayer. **I asked God to show me some Jesus…and you walked right in. I prayed to God to prove it. Prove Jesus is here for me. That's what I said. Wow."**

* * * * * * * * *

We're not so different from Blake and Gene. We spend a lot of time looking for proof of God's real presence in our lives and in the world around us. Even if we steadfastly believe God is present, even if we strongly believe the Holy Spirit will guide and strengthen us, even if we know in our bones that Jesus is the Messiah, the One who saves us, still **we yearn for glimpses of proof.** We need continuing, real, and profound evidence that 'Jesus stuff' is active and at work in our world.

Scripture shows us that the official believed...something. He *begged* Jesus to help him. We *beg* when we believe what we are *begging* for is possible. Otherwise, why waste the tremendous energy required to *beg*? The official had a plan: Jesus would come, probably lay hands on his son, and heal him. The official had already defined the proof he was looking for. Jesus didn't, and doesn't today, submit to human expectations and definitions.

The 'proof' the official received was beyond amazing. Our lives aren't so different...

* * * * * * * * *

Reflections...

What would you say to Blake?

How is Gene answering Blake's challenge to "prove it!"?

How would you describe Gene's ministry? Where do you think he gets the courage to step into that ministry?

Where and how do you look for God's (Christ's, the Holy Spirit's) presence in your life?

Reflections (continued)

How might your expectations of God's (Christ's, the Holy Spirit's) appearance and work limit how much of that presence you are able to experience and/or notice?

If someone were looking for proof of 'Jesus stuff', where and how would you advise them to search?

20

Power in the Margins

After this there was a Jewish festival, and Jesus went up to Jerusalem. In Jerusalem near the Sheep Gate in the north city wall is a pool with the Aramaic name Bethsaida. It had five covered porches, and a crowd of people who were sick, blind, lame, and paralyzed sat there. **A certain man was there who had been sick for thirty-eight years.** *When Jesus saw him lying there, knowing that he had already been there a long time, He asked him,* **"Do you want to get well?"**

The sick man answered Him, **"Sir, I don't have anyone who can put me in the water** *when it is stirred up. When I'm trying to get to it, someone else has gotten in ahead of me."*

Jesus said to him, "Get up! Pick up your mat and walk. **Immediately the man was well, and he picked up his mat and walked. Now that day was the Sabbath.**

The Jewish leaders said to the man who had been healed, "It's the Sabbath; you aren't allowed to carry your mat." He answered, "The man who made me well said to me, "Pick up your mat and walk."

They inquired, "Who is this man who said to you, 'Pick it up and walk'?" The man who had been cured didn't know who it was, because Jesus had slipped away from the crowd gathered there. - John 5:1-13, Common English Bible

Soon another Feast came around and Jesus was back in Jerusalem. Near the Sheep Gate in Jerusalem there was a pool, in Hebrew called Bethesda, with five alcoves. Hundreds of sick people – blind, crippled, paralyzed – were in these alcoves. **One man had been an invalid there for thirty-eight years.** *When Jesus saw him stretched out by the pool and knew how long he had been there, He said,* **"Do you want to get well?"**

The sick man said, **"Sir, when the water is stirred, I don't have anybody to put me in the pool.** *By the time I get there, somebody else is already in."*

Jesus said, "Get up, take your bedroll, start walking." **The man was healed on the spot. He picked up his bedroll and walked off. That day happened to be the Sabbath.**

The Jews stopped the healed man and said, "It's the Sabbath. You can't carry your bedroll around. It's against the rules." But he told them, "The man who made me well told me to. He said, 'Take your bedroll and start walking.'"

They asked, "Who gave you the order to take it up and start walking?" But the healed man didn't know, for Jesus had slipped away into the crowd. - John 5:1-13, The Message Version

* * * * * * * * * *

It was a crazy night in the local emergency room. The thick coat of ice left by evening sleet and freezing rain was immediately followed by a rare late spring blizzard, which had already dumped almost a foot of snow. Thanks to winds still gusting over thirty miles an hour, more snow blew in with every opening of the emergency department doors.

Casualties of the storm had been arriving in astonishing numbers for almost twelve hours, and the staff was exhausted. Exam rooms full, those not able to wait in the waiting room (which was full to overflowing anyway) were lined up end to end on hospital gurneys which lined every hallway.

Bart looked around from his spot on the gurney. They'd parked him at the end of the hall next to the swinging doors leading to the emergency surgery unit. Each time he almost dozed off, the doors would swing open, bumping solidly into him. No one seemed to notice. In fact, only two people had even made eye contact with him in the two hours he'd been parked at the end of the hall. They just kept zipping by. No one talked to him. No one checked on him. **Bart prayed he wouldn't have to go to the bathroom.** He knew that as dizzy and weak as he was, he would never make it by himself. As he lay there, he wished he hadn't lost Rita, his beloved wife of over fifty years. He just felt so alone and helpless. **And they just kept zipping by.....**

Wow. Just wow. New to "big city" residency, Tim (Dr. Tim Asman) hurried down the emergency room hallway. This was quite different from his first residency in the small town hospital down south! Patients kept pouring through the doors. At the same time, ambulances seemed to arrive in a never-ending stream, mostly bringing the results of foolish people attempting to drive on the blizzard-over-ice streets and highways running into one another and/or objects larger than their vehicles.

As Tim passed through the emergency surgery doors yet one more time, he noticed the old man on the gurney by the doors. Again. **That guy must have been there at least a couple of hours.** Tim looked down at him and smiled. Saying a quick "Be with you soon." he hurried by. Tim tried to focus on the patient chart in front of him, but **he kept seeing the old man's eyes.** They'd looked so sad, so helpless, so hopeless. He turned to Willa, one of the nurses. "What's the deal with the guy right by the doors?". Willa rolled her eyes. **"You'll get used to it, doctor. This is the big city, and he's just one more poor old guy with no insurance.** He's not bleeding out, nothing broken far as we can tell, so he waits. All he's got is medicare, so he waits. Just the way it is."

Tim tried again. "But he looks weaker and more out of it every time I pass by. What's his issue?" Willa rolled her eyes. "No time now, doctor. Got to get back to it." Shaking her head, she grabbed a patient chart and walked away.

Tim thought of his grandpa. He completed his note in the chart and made up his mind. Tim walked back through the swinging doors into the emergency department, careful not to bump the old man's temporary bed with the door, and stopped next to him. **"Sir? Sir, are you awake?"**

Bart opened his eyes. Was he seeing things? He looked up into Tim's worried face. "You a doctor?"

Concerned at the length of time it took the old guy to respond, Tim reached out to shake hands, noting the great difficulty the old man had in even lifting his hand. He patted him on the arm. "It's OK, sir. I'm Dr. Asman. What problems are you having?"

"Name's Bart. Bart Johnson. Strangest thing. Getting weaker and weaker. Got my meds in my pocket. Took 'em just like it says. Took some more a half hour or so ago, just like the label said I should...**been waiting here a long time...no one stops. They keep whizzing by me**...busy with sicker....people....I....guess...." His voice drifted to silence.

Tim looked in Bart's eyes. Not good. He reached in Bart's pocket and found the prescription bottle nestled there. His eyes grew wider as he read the dosage and instructions. **Four of these every <u>two</u> hours? No way. At this guy's age, he'd be dead soon at this rate!** Tim quickly retrieved an IV kit, pole, and bag of hydration fluids. "Hang in there, Mr. Johnson. I think we caught this in time. Your med instructions are wrong. Sir?" Tim set the flow on the IV pump to flush Bart's system out. "I'll be right back, sir. I think we've got this figured out."

No wonder Bart was sick. Lucky he wasn't dead. An hour later, a much revived Bart left the emergency room, corrected medication instructions in hand (<u>Two</u> pills every <u>four</u> hours). As he left, one of the nurses asked him which doctor made the decision to "jump him in line". She sternly informed him, **"That's not how we do things around here."**

Not a surprise to Bart….

(to be continued in next chapter….)

* * * * * * * * *

*"The sick man answered Him, **"Sir, I don't have anyone who can put me in the water** when it is stirred up. When I'm trying to get to it, someone else has gotten in ahead of me." (Jn 5:7)*

Bart lay virtually helpless on that gurney as others "zipped" and "whisked" by him. After a while it became obvious that it wasn't just those who were more seriously injured or hurt that were being attended to before him (which was completely understandable). He noted that many others who were far less urgently ill than he was (but had insurance and/or money to pay) received attention as he lay in the hallway, his portable bed often whacked hard by the swinging emergency surgery door. **This kind of priority-setting occurs quite often in many different settings:** hospitals and clinics, but also restaurants, transit services, and retail environments, to name a few.

"They inquired, "Who is this man who said to you, 'Pick it up and walk'?" The man who had been cured didn't know who it was, because Jesus had slipped away from the crowd gathered there." (Jn 5:12)

It would seem logical that praise would be due those who notice the Bart Johnsons of the world. Even though a few (such as Mother Teresa) are made famous for their advocacy for the ignored and forgotten, many risk job loss, public criticism, and/or ostracism for their insistence in standing in solidarity with marginalized sisters and brothers.

* * * * * * * * *

Reflections...

Have you or someone you know been in a situation like Bart Johnson? If no help came, what was that like? If someone stepped up to advocate for you/them, even if the situation wasn't resolved, what difference did that make?

Jesus shows us that following Him means opening our eyes to those who are marginalized, sharing His "power in the margins". What causes us to ignore/overlook such persons?

While it is true that one person cannot effectively empower all those "in the margins", each of us has gifts, talents, and resources to aid someone(s). Take a moment to think of the places you regularly find yourself. Choose one in which you will intentionally improve your awareness of those around you who are often ignored and marginalized. Perhaps it will be as simple as noticing a cashier or restaurant server's name and using it as you interact with him/her.

In what venue is Christ calling you to share His "power in the margins"?

21

Holy Work

*Later Jesus found him in the temple and said to him, "See, you have been made well! Do not sin anymore, so that nothing worse happens to you." **The man went away and told the Jews that it was Jesus who had made him well. Therefore the Jews started persecuting Jesus, because He was doing such things on the Sabbath.***

***But Jesus answered them, "My Father is still working, and I also am working."** For this reason the Jews were seeking all the more to kill Him, because He was not only breaking the Sabbath, but was also calling God His own Father, thereby making Himself equal to God.*

Jesus said to them, "Very truly, I tell you, the Son can do nothing on His own, but only what He sees the Father doing; for whatever the Father does, the Son does likewise. The Father loves the Son and shows Him all that He himself is doing; and He will show Him greater works than these, so that you will be astonished. Indeed, just as the Father raises the dead and gives them life, so also the Son gives life to whomever He wishes.

*The Father judges no one but has given all judgment to the Son, so that all may honor the Son just as they honor the Father. **Anyone who does not honor the Son does not honor the Father who sent Him.***

- John 5:14-23, New Revised Standard Version

*Later, Jesus met the man in the Temple and told him, "You are now well. But don't sin anymore or something worse might happen to you." **The man left and told the leaders that Jesus was the one who had healed him. They started making a lot of trouble for Jesus because He did things like this on the Sabbath.***

***But Jesus said, "My Father has never stopped working, and this is why I keep on working."** Now the leaders wanted to kill Jesus for two reasons. First, He had broken the law of the Sabbath. But even worse, He had said God was His Father, which made Him equal with God.*

Jesus told the people: "I tell you for certain the Son cannot do anything on His own. He can do only what He sees the Father doing, and He does exactly what He sees the Father do. The Father loves the Son and has shown Him everything He does. The Father will show Him even greater things, and you will be amazed. Just as the Father raises the dead and gives life, so the Son gives life to anyone He wants to.

*The Father doesn't judge anyone, but He has made His Son the judge of everyone. The Father wants all people to honor the Son as much as they honor Him. **When anyone refuses to honor the Son, this is the same as refusing to honor the Father who sent Him.***

- John 5:14-23, Contemporary English Version

* * * * * * * * * *

(story continued from last chapter....)

"Name's Bart. Bart Johnson. Strangest thing. Getting weaker and weaker. Got my meds in my pocket. Took 'em just like it says. Took some more a half hour or so ago, just like the label said I should...been waiting here a long time...no one stops. They keep whizzing by me...busy with sicker....people....I....guess...." His voice drifted to silence.

Dr. Tim Asman looked in Bart's eyes. Not good. He reached in Bart's pocket and found the prescription bottle nestled there. His eyes grew wider as he read the dosage and instructions. **Four of these every <u>two</u> hours? No way. At this guy's age, he'd be dead soon at this rate!** Tim quickly retrieved an IV kit, pole, and bag of hydration fluids. "Hang in there, Mr. Johnson. I think we caught this in time. Your med instructions are wrong. Sir?" Tim set the flow on the IV pump to flush Bart's system out. "I'll be right back, sir. I think we've got this figured out."

No wonder Bart was sick. Lucky he wasn't dead. **An hour later, a much revived Bart left the emergency room,** corrected medication instructions in hand (<u>Two</u> pills every <u>four</u> hours). As he left, one of the nurses had asked him which doctor made the decision to "jump him in line". She sternly informed him, **"That's not how we do things around here."** Not a surprise to Bart....

As he took his regular walk in the park a few days later (in warmer weather), Dr. Asman saw Bart. "Hey, Mr. Johnson, how are you doing? Feeling better?" Bart smiled. "Sure am, Doc. Thanks so much for helping me. Something odd though, suppose you should know. **Don't think those clinic folks like you much.** Wouldn't be surprised much if they don't make trouble for you, not at all. They asked me who you were, and **I told them, said you were the best.** Thought you should know. **Hope they don't make trouble for you, but**...they have their rules and such, you know?" Bart shrugged, smiled, and waved as he walked away.

That afternoon Dr. Asman received a text message. **Would he please stop by the Hospital clinic as soon as possible?** *Oh boy, here it comes.* Tim was grateful to Bart for the heads-up warning as he headed for the clinic administrator's office. As he walked through the clinic doors, the administrator met him. "Hello, Dr. Asman. Come on back. Just **need to talk to you, won't take long."** *Man, this can't be good...*

"Tim, I know you're new here to the city and all, but....well, **we have policies and procedures. Did you get a copy of the manual?** Tim nodded 'yes' in answer. "Good, well, be sure to read it, especially the section on triage. Unless they're bleeding, have broken bones, or are having a cardiac event, **no insurance and no money means they wait. Got it?"**

Tim noticed the beautiful cross necklace the administrator wore. He took a deep breath. "Not to be too personal, but I noticed the lovely cross necklace you're wearing. Why do you wear it?" A confused look crossed the clinic administrator's face. **"Well, it's because I'm a Christian. I go to church.** I know you're busy, so I'll let you go. Just remember, Tim: policies and procedures – we have them for a reason."

As Tim walked out the clinic doors, he pulled the keychain his dad had given him from his pocket and read the words on it: 'Whenever you did it to the least of these, you did it to me...' – Jesus" How could he act counter to that? He couldn't, and he decided he wouldn't.

So Dr. Tim Osman was assigned nights, weekends, and holidays...all of them. The least desirable shifts. At first, it bothered him. Then he discovered the irony of it all. These were the very days and times which those others overlooked, ignored, and marginalized were most likely to come to the emergency department for help. Several days later, Tim smiled as he bowed his head in a quick prayer at the beginning of yet another midnight shift. "Thank you, God, for this opportunity for another 'Holy Work' assignment. Thank you for choosing me as one of your 'Holy Workers'. Amen." **...and another shift of Holy Work began...**

* * * * * * * * * *

"The man went away and told the Jews that it was Jesus who had made him well. Therefore the Jews started persecuting Jesus, because He was doing such things on the Sabbath. But Jesus answered them, 'My Father is still working, and I also am working.' For this reason the Jews were seeking all the more to kill Him,..." (Jn 5:15-17)

Policies and procedures are important. At their best, their purpose is to ensure fairness, efficiency, and high-quality results. At their worst, they can be instruments of ensuring status, privilege, and unjustified preferential treatment.

Jesus makes the point that structures we put in place should have the **priority purpose** of doing the work of God – all the time. As we watch and learn from Jesus, we learn there is no day or time absent from godly priorities - which place no person above any other. **God is always at work!**

* * * * * * * * * *

Reflections...

What are the times, places, and situations in which it is easiest for you to practice the godly priorities Jesus demonstrates here? What is your 'Holy Work"?

How does your life reflect the priorities of the clinic administrator? Why do you think that is? What will you do about it?

22

A New Day is HERE!

"I tell you the truth, those who listen to my message and believe in God who sent me have eternal life. They will never be condemned for their sins, but they have already passed from death into life.

*"And **I assure you that the time is coming, indeed it's here now, when the dead will hear my voice-- the voice of the Son of God. And those who listen will live.** The Father has life in himself, and he has granted that same life-giving power to his Son. And he has given him authority to judge everyone because he is the Son of Man.*

"Don't be so surprised! Indeed, the time is coming when all the dead in their graves will hear the voice of God's Son, and they will rise again. Those who have done good will rise to experience eternal life, and those who have continued in evil will rise to experience judgment.

"I can do nothing on my own. I judge as God tells me. Therefore, my judgment is just, because I carry out the will of the one who sent me, not my own will. If I were to testify on my own behalf, my testimony would not be valid. But someone else is also testifying about me, and I assure you that everything he says about me is true. In fact, you sent investigators to listen to John the Baptist, and his testimony about me was true.

*"Of course, **I have no need of human witnesses, but I say these things so you might be saved.***

"John was like a burning and shining lamp, and you were excited for a while about his message. But I have a greater witness than John-- my teachings and my miracles. The Father gave me these works to accomplish, and they prove that he sent me.   *- John 5:24-36, New Living Translation*

"It's urgent that you listen carefully to this: Anyone here who believes what I am saying right now and aligns himself with the Father, who has in fact put me in charge, has at this very moment the real, lasting life and is no longer condemned to be an outsider. This person has taken a giant step from the world of the dead to the world of the living."

*"It's urgent that you get this right: **The time has arrived – I mean right now! – when dead men and women will hear the voice of the Son of God and, hearing, will come alive.** Just as the Father has life in Himself, he has conferred on the Son life in Himself. And He has given Him the authority, simply because He is the Son of Man, to decide and carry out matters of judgment.*

"Don't act so surprised at all this. The time is coming when everyone dead and buried will hear His voice. Those who have lived the right way will walk out into a resurrection life; those who have lived the wrong way, into a resurrection judgment.

"I can't do a solitary thing on my own: I listen, then I decide. You can trust my decision because I'm not out to get my own way but only to carry out orders. If I were simply speaking on my own account, it would be an empty, self-serving

witness. But an independent witness confirms me, the most reliable Witness of all. Furthermore, you all saw and heard John, and he gave expert and reliable testimony about me, didn't he?

*"But **my purpose is not to get your vote, and not to appeal to mere human testimony. I'm speaking to you this way so that you will be saved.***

John was a torch, blazing and bright, and you were glad enough to dance for an hour or so in his bright light. But the witness that really confirms me far exceeds John's witness. It's the work the Father gave me to complete. These very tasks, as I go about completing them, confirm that the Father, in fact, sent me.

- John 5:24-36, The Message Version

* * * * * * * * * *

What a choice. **Caught with drugs in his school locker, the judge gave Brent a choice:** a nine month juvie (youth detention) sentence....or 400 hours of community service at the new drug rehab house for youth and a transfer to the alternative high school for the rest of the year. Some choice.

Brent chose freedom, so here he sat in the common area of the "Death to Life House". Some name – made him look around for walking zombies or something...weird. Stupid rules too; he'd had to check in his phone at the front desk before they'd let him in.

Lost in his own thoughts, Brent was startled by a voice next to him. "Hey, name's Mike. What's yours?" Brent looked up. "Um...Brent. Name's Brent."

"Well, Brent, you new here? I've been here a month, since they opened this place. Want me to show you the ropes around here? It's not that bad, really."

Brent looked up. Something about this guy made him open up. "Hi Mike. Honestly? **Judge gave me a bunch of community service hours here. That or juvie. Some choice; I chose this."**

"Cool. Well, probably not cool what got you here, but cool that you're here. This is a good place. Weird name, though, huh, 'Death to Life House'. **Thought maybe I'd see a bunch of druggie zombies running around, you know?"** Both laughed as they mimed walking zombies.

Then Mike suddenly got serious. "That's not far off the truth though. Just depends on what choices you make. **I had two roommates when I first moved in.** The three of us were the first residents. Jared had this thing he'd say all the time: when he got up, before meals, when he went to bed....he even worked up a tune for it. Over and over and over....at first it drove me crazy! Then I got used to it. Now I can hear it even though he's not here so much anymore. He's moving out next week – going to college, go figure!"

Brent was really curious now. **"What was it? What did he keep saying?"**

"OK, here it is: **'A new day is HERE!'. That's it.** One day I asked him about it. He pointed at the house sign, told me to read it carefully. Then he just walked away."

Brent hadn't noticed much about the house sign, other than the weirdness of it. Maybe he'd have to take a closer look later. Mike began speaking again. "Then there's Leon. Leon, well, Leon chose the road from 'Death' to what you could call 'Deader'. He threw his life away, went back to the streets. Three days here, he started sneaking out, back to running drugs. And, duh, got caught. Just like you said, juvie's not a lot of fun. Not at all. Well, gotta go so I'm not late for my new job. They helped me get a spot working at the coffee shop. Can't let 'em down; can't let myself down either. See ya round."

As Mike walked away, Brent wandered back out front to read the **"fine print" on the house sign.**   This is what he saw in the 'fine print' under the house name: *"And **I assure you that the time is coming, indeed it's here now, when the dead will hear my voice - the voice of the Son of God. And those who listen will live.** –John 5:25"*

Mike's quote from his roommate Jared ran through his mind, and he smiled. **"A new day is HERE!"** Brent made up his mind then and there. Like Jared, he was going to claim his "New Day". He was going to choose "Death to Life"; there would be no "Death to Deader" for him!

* * * * * * * * *

Jared understood. Mike got it. The life choices they had made were taking them in the wrong direction – fast, and the finish line coming into sight was definitely not the one they wanted to cross. Jared and Mike made the choice to turn around. **They chose life over death.** But it was more than that. Jared went to college. Mike had a new mission. He made it a point to greet new guys coming to the "Death to Life House" and point them to the "fine print" of the house sign. Then he handed them a card which said this:

*"It's urgent that you listen carefully to this: Anyone here who believes what I am saying right now and aligns himself with the Father, who has in fact put me in charge, has at this very moment the real, lasting life and is no longer condemned to be an outsider. **This person has taken a giant step from the world of the dead to the world of the living."** – John 5:24*

As Brent spent more time serving at the "Death to Life House", he met more young men. Some chose new life; others chose the way of death and left for the streets, juvenile detention, or jail. He **got curious and looked up the Scripture quoted on the house sign.** As he faced challenges to return to his old life selling drugs, these words of Jesus anchored him on the journey from "death to life": *"But my purpose is not to get your vote, and not to appeal to mere human testimony. I'm speaking to you this way so that you will be saved." (John 5:34)*

* * * * * * * * *

Reflections...

In what ways is your life most aligned with God, showing Christ in charge?

Reflections (continued)

Think about the areas of your life which present you with the most challenges and temptations to choose the "way of death", away from alignment with a life of discipleship to Christ. What resources can you lean on to strengthen you in those battles? Are you using them?

Who has God placed in your life for whom you can serve as Mike did in the above story? What are you doing about it?

23

Living in Worship

"And the Father who sent me testifies about me. You have never even heard his voice or seen his form, and you don't have his word dwelling with you because you don't believe the one whom he has sent.

"Examine the scriptures, since you think that in them you have eternal life. They also testify about me, yet you don't want to come to me so that you can have life.

"I don't accept praise from people, but I know you, that you don't have God's love in you. I have come in my Father's name, and you don't receive me. If others come in their own name, you receive them. How can you believe when you receive praise from each other but don't seek the praise that comes from the only God?

"Don't think that I will accuse you before the Father. Your accuser is Moses, the one in whom your hope rests. If you believed Moses, you would believe me, because Moses wrote about me. If you don't believe the writings of Moses, how will you believe my words?"

- John 5:37-47, Common English Bible

"The Father who sent me, confirmed me. And you missed it. You never heard His voice, you never saw His appearance. There is nothing left in your memory of His message because you do not take His Messenger seriously."

"You have your heads in your Bibles constantly because you think you'll find eternal life there. But you miss the forest for the trees. These Scriptures are all about me! And here I am, standing right before you, and you aren't willing to receive from me the life you say you want.

"I'm not interested in crowd approval. And do you know why? Because I know you and your crowds. I know that love, especially God's love, is not on your working agenda. I came with the authority of my Father, and you either dismiss me or avoid me. If another came, acting self-important, you would welcome him with open arms. How do you expect to get anywhere with God when you spend all your time jockeying for position with each other, ranking your rivals and ignoring God?

"But don't think I'm going to accuse you before my Father. Moses, in whom you put so much stock, is your accuser. If you believed, really believed, what Moses said, you would believe me. He wrote of me. If you won't take seriously what he wrote, how can I expect you to take seriously what I speak?"

- John 5:37-47, The Message Version

* * * * * * * * * *

Listen in to this conversation between members of a church leadership team and a consultant hired to help them strengthen and grow the congregation:

"But we're doing all the right things...!"

"Why?" (consultant)

"Maybe we need some new programs..."

"Why?" (consultant)

"Perhaps a new worship time, or different music, or..."

"Why?" (consultant)

"Why do you keep asking us 'Why'?"

"Why do you think?" (consultant)

"Well, maybe you want us to think...and check to see if our reasons for doing what we're doing still make sense...?"

"What do you want to do?" (consultant)

"Grow the church. We need more people...and more money. The budget is a mess!"

"So what you want is more people and more money, right?" (consultant)

"That's what Sally just said – people and money. Young people. Kids. So we need better fundraisers and programs."

"What does God want you to do?" (consultant)

(silence, confused looks) "What?"

"Yes, what? What do you think God wants you to do?" (consultant)

"Well, if the church is going to make it, we need money and young people. This discussion isn't getting anywhere. Do you have ideas for us...or not?"

"Oh, I have ideas. But maybe the problem is your starting line. Think about it: where did the whole "church" begin? It's not the 'body of fundraising' or the 'body of good programs'. It's the..." (consultant)

(team member, interrupting) "...the Body of <u>Christ</u>! So if it's His body here on earth, what you're saying is that it's about what He wants, not us. Is that it?"

"Here's something to think about: **Do you want to be known as 'church-ians' ... or Christ-ians?"** (consultant)

"Huh?"

"'Church-ians' ask what they want, which strategies will get them what they want, and they rejoice when they get what they want. 'Christ-ians' ask what God wants, what strategies will accomplish what God wants, and they rejoice when God's desires are met." (consultant)

"I get it. So we have to look at who we are, apart and together as church, and look around us to see who, what, where, and how God is calling us to make a difference for Christ right here and now. Is that it?"

"Don't forget the 'why?' question. Always check yourself with that. Are you living in worship, or just living to survive?" (consultant)

"Living in worship….living in worship…I like that. Seems Jesus' whole life was about exactly that. He lived, and died…in worship."

The congregation was never the same again. As they shifted from being survival-focused 'church-ians' and became more and more 'Christ-ians' – the Body of Christ in the community – they blossomed. They began to learn how to live every day, each moment…in worship!

* * * * * * * * *

"I'm not interested in crowd approval. And do you know why? Because I know you and your crowds. **I know that love, especially God's love, is not on your working agenda.** *I came with the authority of my Father, and you either dismiss me or avoid me.* (Jn 5:41-42)

Many of us get so wrapped up in the mechanics of church life that we gradually lose our focus on the "Why" of being church in the first place! Whether we are on the "inside" or "outside" of church life (and many are somewhere in between), we get too busy with the "what, when, how, and where" factors that we lose sight of the most important, focus-guiding question we must continually answer: **"Why?" Why church at all? What is the church, called the Body of Christ in Scripture, supposed to be about?**

"You have your heads in your Bibles constantly because you think you'll find eternal life there. But you miss the forest for the trees. **These Scriptures are all about** *me***! And here I am, standing right before you, and you aren't willing to receive from me the life you say you want.** (Jn. 5:39-40)

Many times, our intentions are good. We tell ourselves that we're all about sharing the Good News of Jesus. The problem comes when our actions stray from that core purpose. **What was Jesus all about?** He met people where they were – but refused to leave them there. He was all about showing them eternity – an amazing eternity lived in God's presence and glory! Scripture doesn't really dwell too much on specifics of fundraising or programming. It's much more like this: **Go! Share! Live in Worship!**

* * * * * * * * *

Reflections…

If you are part of a congregation, take a moment to think: How much focus, resources, worry, are spent on the 'mechanics' of being church? In other words, what about your congregation is more 'church-ian'?

Reflections (continued)

If you are not part of a congregation, when you think of 'church' and 'church-people', what images come to mind? Where does their focus seem to be?

Whether you are part of a congregation or not, why do you think the church exists?

What is the difference between a 'church-ian' and a 'Christ-ian'?

Which do you think the earliest disciples were? Which would you rather be? What are you doing about that?

24

Leftovers...?

After this, Jesus crossed over to the far side of the Sea of Galilee, also known as the Sea of Tiberias. A huge crowd kept following him wherever he went, because they saw his miraculous signs as he healed the sick. Then Jesus climbed a hill and sat down with his disciples around him. (It was nearly time for the Jewish Passover celebration.)

Jesus soon saw a huge crowd of people coming to look for him. Turning to Philip, he asked, "Where can we buy bread to feed all these people?" He was testing Philip, for he already knew what he was going to do.

Philip replied, "Even if we worked for months, we wouldn't have enough money to feed them!" Then Andrew, Simon Peter's brother, spoke up. "There's a young boy here with five barley loaves and two fish. But what good is that with this huge crowd?"

"Tell everyone to sit down," Jesus said. So they all sat down on the grassy slopes. (The men alone numbered 5,000.) Then Jesus took the loaves, gave thanks to God, and distributed them to the people. Afterward he did the same with the fish. And they all ate as much as they wanted.

After everyone was full, Jesus told his disciples, **"Now gather the leftovers, so that nothing is wasted." So they picked up the pieces and filled twelve baskets with scraps left by the people who had eaten from the five barley loaves.**
- John 6:1-13, New Living Translation

After this Jesus went to the other side of the Sea of Galilee, also called the Sea of Tiberias. A large crowd kept following him, because they saw the signs that he was doing for the sick. Jesus went up the mountain and sat down there with his disciples. Now the Passover, the festival of the Jews, was near.

When he looked up and saw a large crowd coming toward him, Jesus said to Philip, "Where are we to buy bread for these people to eat?" He said this to test him, for he himself knew what he was going to do.

Philip answered him, "Six months' wages would not buy enough bread for each of them to get a little." One of his disciples, Andrew, Simon Peter's brother, said to him, "There is a boy here who has five barley loaves and two fish. But what are they among so many people?"

Jesus said, "Make the people sit down." Now there was a great deal of grass in the place; so they sat down, about five thousand in all. Then Jesus took the loaves, and when he had given thanks, he distributed them to those who were seated; so also the fish, as much as they wanted.

When they were satisfied, he told his disciples, **"Gather up the fragments left over, so that nothing may be lost." So they gathered them up, and from the fragments of the five barley loaves, left by those who had eaten, they filled twelve baskets.**
- John 6:1-13, New Revised Standard Version

* * * * * * * * *

Amy was amazed. **It was her very first time helping prepare and serve food at the downtown 'soup kitchen', but she was discovering that much more than soup was involved.** She had met some good cooks, but these people were simply amazing! They took whatever food was donated and turned it into fabulous (and plentiful) meals. As she stood in the dining are looking through the large serving window into the kitchen, it looked like a well-orchestrated cooking ballet was in progress. Amy looked up to see her best friend Stacy smiling at her. "So Amy, what do you think?" **"Wow," was all Amy could think to say. "Just wow."**

Stacy pointed at the outside doors. "Just wait till all the people come through those doors. We'll probably feed over 200 people today."

"Two hundred? Seriously?" Amy pictured what that would look like. "Two hundred people? Those kitchen people aren't just good. They're awesome! **Two hundred people fed with…leftovers…simply amazing."**

Stacy smiled again. "Oh, and **that's not the end of the story either.** After that, we'll pack up all those meal leftovers and take them to the homeless camps down by the river. And Tom (he's the one making the veggies) discovered another group camping in the old warehouse down by the abandoned railroad tracks. Our motto truly is: **There are no leftovers. No leftovers with Jesus, so no leftovers with His disciples (that's us) either. That's why we call it the "No Leftovers Ministry".**

* * * * * * * * *

We are a culture which seems irresistably drawn to fantastic, sensational, over-the-top spectacles. Whether in the news or on so-called 'reality shows', we are tempted (many times successfully) and drawn to give these events all our attention.

While all our attention is on the "miracle", Jesus' attention shifts to great care toward the *leftovers*… We tend to overlook the very things Jesus focuses on. Here's the "end of the story" again: *"After everyone was full, Jesus told his disciples, 'Now gather the leftovers, so that nothing is wasted.' So they picked up the pieces and filled twelve baskets with scraps left by the people who had eaten from the five barley loaves."* (Jn 6:12-13)

Twelve tribes of Israel. Twelve disciples. And twelve baskets of "leftovers". Twelve. Jesus is teaching us something here. **God takes what people consider leftovers, expendable, not worthy of further attention – and builds a nation** (twelve tribes), a foundation for the spread of the Good News (twelve disciples), and now…now He connects these twelve baskets of "leftovers" to that tradition in order to make the point that **not only is nothing wasted, but God builds His Kingdom from that which the world would discard as unworthy and useless.**

* * * * * * * * *

Reflections...

Like most, your attention is probably drawn to the amazing miracle Jesus performed to feed all those people (5,000 men plus women and children). Only God could accomplish such a thing! But what about the "rest of the story" – the ending? How do you think they are connected?

As Stacy shared the meaning of the feeding ministry, "No Leftovers Ministry", what were your thoughts?

What / Who do we throw out as "leftover" which this Scripture teaches is needed (and perhaps even vital) to keep, use, and even build a future on?

25

Storm Surge

When the people saw that he had done a miraculous sign, they said, "This is truly the prophet who is coming into the world." **Jesus understood that they were about to come and force him to be their king, so he took refuge again, alone on a mountain.**

When evening came, Jesus' disciples went down to the lake. They got into a boat and were crossing the lake to Capernaum. It was already getting dark and Jesus hadn't come to them yet. The water was getting rough because a strong wind was blowing. When the wind had driven them out for about three or four miles, they saw Jesus walking on the water.

He was approaching the boat and they were afraid. He said to them, "I Am. Don't be afraid." Then they wanted to take him into the boat, and just then the boat reached the land where they had been heading.
- John 6:14-21, Common English Bible

The people realized that God was at work among them in what Jesus had just done. They said, "This is the Prophet for sure, God's Prophet right here in Galilee!" **Jesus saw that in their enthusiasm, they were about to grab Him and make Him king, so He slipped off and went back up the mountain to be by Himself.**

In the evening His disciples went down to the sea, got in the boat, and headed back across the water to Capernaum. It had grown quite dark and Jesus had not yet returned. A huge wind blew up, churning the sea. They were maybe three or four miles out when they saw Jesus walking on the sea, quite near the boat.

They were scared senseless, but He reassured them, "It's me. It's all right. Don't be afraid." So they took Him on board. In no time they reached land – the exact spot they were headed to.   *- John 5:14-21, The Message Version*

* * * * * * * * *

"Wow! I can't believe we made it!" George stepped out into his yard from the basement to find his neighbor Joe surveying the wind and hail damage to his home. "Well, I guess you could say that, but **I think I'm finally gonna have to get a new roof.** But I guess you're right, George. With the coast just a quarter-mile down the road, it could have been a lot worse..."

George paused in his branch picking up duties. "Yep, we came out A-OK. Hey, you and Betty want to go out with us to dinner? Might as well celebrate our good fortune."

Joe looked up at the sky. **"Well, this hurricane, you know it's not done with us yet, right?** I know you just moved here from Michigan and all, but you do know about the surge, don't you?"

"The what?" George looked again at Joe's face. Was Joe kidding? Surge? What?

"Surge. As in storm surge. As in water flooding in up to your neck, George. The worst of this is probably still coming. Soon."

George looked closer at Joe's van. It looked…loaded with stuff. Just then Joe's wife Betty came out the door of their house carrying little Jamie. "Come on, honey, let's go! The surge'll be here any time. Frank and LaShawnda are already at the shelter. We've got to go!"

Two hours later, George was really grateful for neighbors like Joe and Betty. With his wife Cheryl out of town on a business trip (and worried frantic about them), he'd had just enough time to gather necessary supplies, clothes, and their two young children before the police and firefighters started coming down their street ordering evacuation.

Two days later, George, Joe, and their families returned to begin cleaning out and repairing their flooded homes. **The storm surge came, all right, four feet of water invading** all the homes on their block. During those weeks of cleanup and recovery, there were many times when George missed his old home in Michigan… many times.

* * * * * * * * * *

In this Scripture, we are invited to **witness what happened "after the storm" – the storm of need.** Five thousand men, plus women and children, all gathered to hear Jesus – and no food. The disciples were understandably worried! How would Jesus address this tremendous need?

Jesus fed them all – and even had twelve baskets full of leftovers! *Whew!! Glad that's over.* These may have been the disciples' thoughts as they settled in the boat for the trip across the lake to Capernaum. **The storm was over. Jesus brought relief! But why then would He run away just when the people wanted to make Him king? Strange…**

Little did they know (though Jesus certainly did) that the real storm was coming. He was about to demonstrate the importance of preparing for life's "storm surge" times. Jesus went away to a quiet place to pray and renew himself for the coming storms. **Just like the sea retreats from the shore (before the storm surge), Jesus retreats to the mountain to recharge with God.**

As they crossed the sea, the disciples were caught up in a storm. **Just when they thought it should be "smooth sailing" (as we often do), then came the worst of the storm. Jesus was ready,** and He came to them in the midst of the storm to give them what they needed to make it safely to shore. They were so overwhelmed by the storm they didn't even recognize Jesus – the Teacher they'd been traveling with every day!

As we will see in upcoming portions of John's gospel, Jesus continues to prepare the disciples (and us) not just for life's storms, but for the storm surges which often follow. **Like the disciples, once we survive one of life's storms we often forget to spend time allowing God to renew and strengthen us.** We should heed the prophet Isaiah's instruction:

"Have you not known? Have you not heard? The Lord is the everlasting God, the Creator of the ends of the earth. He does not faint or grow weary; his understanding is unsearchable. He gives power to the faint, and strengthens the powerless.

Even youths will faint and be weary, and the young will fall exhausted; but those who wait for the Lord shall renew their strength, they shall mount up with wings like eagles, they shall run and not be weary, they shall walk and not faint."

(40:28-31, New Revised Standard Version).

* * * * * * * * *

Reflections...

Have you ever experienced a "storm after the storm" in your life? If so, what did you learn from the experience?

How is it possible that the disciples in that boat didn't recognize Jesus? How do we have this in common with them?

Why do you think Isaiah found it necessary to give this instruction?

Try putting Isaiah's instructions into your own words, perhaps even fitting it to a situation you face in your own life:

26

What Do You Want?

The next day the crowd that had stayed on the other side of the sea saw that there had been only one boat there. They also saw that Jesus had not got into the boat with his disciples, but that his disciples had gone away alone. Then some boats from Tiberias came near the place where they had eaten the bread after the Lord had given thanks.

So when the crowd saw that neither Jesus nor his disciples were there, they themselves got into the boats and went to Capernaum looking for Jesus. When they found him on the other side of the sea, they said to him, "Rabbi, when did you come here?"

Jesus answered them, "Very truly, I tell you, you are looking for me, not because you saw signs, but because you ate your fill of the loaves. Do not work for the food that perishes, but for the food that endures for eternal life, which the Son of Man will give you. For it is on him that God the Father has set his seal."

Then they said to him, "What must we do to perform the works of God?" Jesus answered them, "This is the work of God, that you believe in him whom he has sent." - *John 6:22-29, New Revised Standard Version*

The people who had stayed on the east side of the lake knew that only one boat had been there. They also knew that Jesus had not left in it with His disciple. But the next day some boats from Tiberius sailed near the place where the crowd had eaten the bread for which the Lord had given thanks.

Then they got into the boats and went to Capernaum to look for Jesus. They found Him on the west side of the lake and asked, "Rabbi, when did you get here?"

"I tell you for certain that you are not looking for me because you saw the miracles, but because you ate all the food you wanted. Don't work for food that spoils. Work for food that gives eternal life. The Son of Man will give you this food, because God the Father has given Him the right to do so."

"What exactly does God want us to do?" *the people asked.* ***Jesus answered, "God wants you to have faith in the One He sent."*** - *John 6:22-29, Contemporary English Version*

* * * * * * * * * *

I invite you to listen in to a conversation I had recently in a local coffee shop. A lady at a nearby table overheard my phone conversation and correctly assumed I had, as she put it, "something to do with church".

She got right to her point. **"I'm Stacy, and we're new in town. Can you help me find the perfect church for us?"**

Perfect church…hmmmm. "Can you tell me a bit more about yourselves?"

Stacy took a deep breath. "Well, to be honest, **we're church-shopping.** We've visited three so far. Nothing yet."

"What did you like most about the churches you've visited?"

"Me and my husband, we have two kids, and one on the way. **The church that can give us the most – that's where we'll stay."She** looked at me expectantly…

Oh my….give them the most…. "When you say 'most', can you help me understand what you mean?"

"Sure. It's pretty simple really, I mean, how hard can it be? Well, for example, **which one has the most free programs where we can leave our kids and go do stuff by ourselves? Some of them even feed the kids for free – now that's not just good value for our donations, that's a bonus!"**

Stacy paused, and once more regarded me expectantly as she reached for her pen and a napkin to write on.

"So you're looking for the most free programs, things like that? Oh, and food for the kids. Anything else?"

"What else is there?"

"Good programs are great, and free food is wonderful, but…."

"Yes?"

"I wonder what else God wants for you. I want to point you in a good direction to plug into that, because, honestly?..." (she nodded, more ready than ever to write) "That's where you'll find what you truly want, even if you don't realize it yet. That's where you'll **find eternal "programs" and free food that never runs out. How would that be?**

"Wow! Now that's the kind of church for us!"

* * * * * * * * *

I saw Stacy in the coffee shop **a few weeks later.** When she saw me, she made a beeline for my table, excitement in her eyes. **"You'll never guess what happened!** The very next Sunday we went to this church. Not the biggest, coolest looking or anything, actually don't know what made us stop there because we were planning to take a break from church hunting that day. We were really headed for the park, but there it was…a church! So we thought, we've got our play clothes on, but hey, let's see what happens. So we parked. We got out of the car. And it happened!"

She was so excited and talking so fast, I was having a hard time keeping up! "What? What happened?"

"Well, first off, friendly people were in the parking lot. One of them, a grandpa-looking guy, helped us corral our three year old. A younger guy helped my husband carry the diaper bag and stuff. Well, you know me, first thing I thought was, this is great and all, but there are friendly greeters at the mall too. But I was definitely interested to see what came next, and **you'll never, ever in a million years believe what it was!"**

"What? What was it, Stacy?" (she definitely had me hooked now!)

"Well, this couple invited us to sit with them, and so I asked her about programs for the kids and all, and do you know what she said? Amazing! She told me: 'Stacy, lots of places have good kids' programs, and you know, you can get free food at the food bank. **What I've found here at this church is the best program ever – God's! And the best free food that never ever runs out – God's! And you know what else, Stacy? I learned that THAT's what I wanted all along. Amazing, isn't it?'** That's what this lady, I think her name was Joan, said to us. Just like you told me a couple weeks ago. Must be a God-thing, huh?"

* * * * * * * * *

Jesus answered them, "Very truly, I tell you, you are looking for me, not because you saw signs, but because you ate your fill of the loaves. Do not work for the food that perishes, but for the food that endures for eternal life, which the Son of Man will give you. For it is on him that God the Father has set his seal."

We're not so different from Stacy or those people by the side of the lake whom Jesus spoke to. We are programmed by the culture around us to be consumers before all else. Slogans like "It's all about you." "You can have it all!" or perhaps "an army of one" train and form us in this attitude and way of living until what we want (we think) is literally what all these marketing folks want us to want!

Jesus seeks to take our life's "GPS" and "recalculate" our journey in radical, life-altering, eternally amazing ways (I call it "<u>G</u>od's <u>P</u>ositioning <u>S</u>ervice"). Our directions are temporary; many times we are blinded to the fact that the destination the world's directions point us to has very little in common with what God wants for us. **The world seeks its own "good". God, with the incredible Gift of Jesus, seeks our true, eternal good.**

Then they said to him, "What must we do to perform the works of God?" Jesus answered them, "This is the work of God, that you believe in him whom he has sent."

That's it? You may ask. Yes, that's it. Allow your belief in, and discipleship to, Christ shape and direct your life. Tune in to God. Listen for the Holy Spirit's direction in your life. Before you know it, God will have "recalculated" your journey of life in incredible ways too. Your answer to "What do you want?" will then more likely resemble what God wants for you…eternal, grace-powered, abundant life!

* * * * * * * * *

Reflections...

What DO you want in life?

Reflections (continued)

How does your answer connect with and/or relate to what the cultural forces around you want?

How does your answer connect or relate to what you think God wants for you?

If you could ask God, "What do You want of me?", what do you imagine God saying?

27

Food for the Journey

They answered, "Show us a miraculous sign if you want us to believe in you. What can you do? After all, our ancestors ate manna while they journeyed through the wilderness! The Scriptures say, 'Moses gave them bread from heaven to eat.'"

Jesus said, "I tell you the truth, Moses didn't give you bread from heaven. My Father did. And now he offers you the true bread from heaven. The true bread of God is the one who comes down from heaven and gives life to the world." **"Sir," they said, "give us that bread every day."**

Jesus replied, **"I am the bread of life. Whoever comes to me will never be hungry again.** *Whoever believes in me will never be thirsty. But you haven't believed in me even though you have seen me. However, those the Father has given me will come to me, and* **I will never reject them.**

For I have come down from heaven to do the will of God who sent me, not to do my own will. **And this is the will of God, that I should not lose even one of all those he has given me, but that I should raise them up at the last day. For it is my Father's will that all who see his Son and believe in him should have eternal life. I will raise them up at the last day."**

Then the people began to murmur in disagreement because he had said, "I am the bread that came down from heaven." They said, "Isn't this Jesus, the son of Joseph? We know his father and mother. How can he say, 'I came down from heaven'?"

But Jesus replied, "Stop complaining about what I said. For no one can come to me unless the Father who sent me draws them to me, and **at the last day I will raise them up.** *As it is written in the Scriptures, 'They will all be taught by God.' Everyone who listens to the Father and learns from him comes to me. (Not that anyone has ever seen the Father; only I, who was sent from God, have seen him.)* **"I tell you the truth, anyone who believes has eternal life.**

- John 6:30-47, New Living Translation

They waffled, "Why don't you give us a clue about who you are, just a hint of what's going on? When we see what's up, we'll commit ourselves. Show us what you can do. Moses fed our ancestors with bread in the desert. It says so in the Scriptures: 'He gave them bread from heaven to eat.'"

Jesus responded, "The real significance of that Scripture is not that Moses gave you bread from heaven but that my Father is right now offering you bread from heaven, the <u>real</u> *bread. The Bread of God came down and is giving life to the world." They jumped at that:* **"Master, give us this bread, now and forever!"**

Jesus said, "I am the Bread of Life. The person who aligns with me hungers no more and thirsts no more, ever. *I have told you this explicitly because even though you have seen me in action, you don't really believe me. Every person the Father gives me eventually comes running to me. And* **once that person is with me, I hold on and don't let go.**

I came down from heaven not to follow my own whim but to accomplish the will of the One who sent me. This, in a nutshell, is that will: that everything handed over to me by the Father be completed – not a single detail missed – and **at the wrap-up of time I have everything and everyone put together, upright and whole. This is what my Father wants: that anyone who sees the Son and trusts who He is and what He does and then aligns with Him will enter _real_ life, _eternal_ life. My part is to put them on their feet alive and whole at the completion of time."**

At this, because He said, "I am the Bread that came down from heaven," the Jews started arguing over Him: "Isn't this the son of Joseph? Don't we know His father? Don't we know His mother? How can He now say, 'I came down out of heaven' and expect anyone to believe Him?"

Jesus said, "Don't bicker among yourselves over me. You're not in charge here. The Father who sent me is in charge. He draws people to me – that's the only way you'll ever come. Only then do I do **my work, putting people together, setting them on their feet, ready for the End.** *This is what the prophets meant when they wrote, 'And then they will all be personally taught by God.'*

Anyone who has spent any time listening to the Father, really listening and therefore learning, comes to me to be taught personally – to see it with his own eyes, hear it with his own ears, from me, since I have it firsthand from the Father. No one has seen the Father except the One who has His Being alongside the Father – and you can see me. "I'm telling you the most solemn and sober truth now: **Whoever believes in me has real life, eternal life.**

- John 6:30-47, The Message Version

* * * * * * * * * *

Stan was so lost in his thoughts as he trimmed the bushes in his front yard that he almost missed young Bobby's departure from the house next door. As he looked a bit closer, he noted that Bobby's backpack looked a little full – well, stuffed would be a better description.

Stan stopped pruning the bushes to wave at Bobby. **Curious, odd even, that the boy was sneaking out the back door…Stan liked Bobby; he was a good kid.** When Stan messed up his back last year, Bobby (just eleven years old then) had stepped up immediately to help. Bobby mowed, raked, trimmed, weeded, took trash out…. he even brought the newspaper to the door every morning on his way to school. And he refused any sort of payment – that about blew Stan's socks off! Yep, a great kid.

Bobby looked troubled today though, so Stan decided to be a little sneaky himself. "Hey, Bobby, think you could spare a few minutes to help me pick up these branches? My back's not what it used to be, you know." As predicted, Bobby hurried over. "You didn't hurt your back again, did you, Mr. Stan?"

"Nope, just tired is all. Thanks so much for stopping to help. **So where are you headed today?**"

Bobby shrugged. **"Out."**

Hmmm…unusual answer for a usually talkative boy. So Stan asked, "Out where?"

"Out there." Bobby pointed off into the distance.

"What's out there?"

(shrug) "Don't know. Stuff."

"Hmmm…'Stuff', eh? Bobby, before you start down a road, be sure you do the very best you can to know where that road goes. So – **where are you going?**"

"Away."

"Best answer yet, 'away'. **Going to find 'a way' where?"**

"Don't know."

"Exactly, Bobby…exactly."

As Stan and Bobby sat on Stan's front porch, the story spilled out. His dad had lost his job of 23 years. Mom was disabled and couldn't work. He overheard his dad talking about all their bills, so **Bobby decided to leave. After all, kids were expensive, he knew that, and maybe without him there, his folks could keep their house.** The youngest of four sons, he had overheard them talking about selling the house and getting something smaller and less expensive after Bobby went to college. Maybe if he left sooner….

As they talked, Stan helped Bobby see the importance of planning a journey before starting one. He shared his own "running away" story – Stan got upset with his dad one day…and ran away to join the Army. It was 1944. Stan shared his own lessons of journey and destination planning. **"No matter what, always have your eye on your goal. Then you'll know what to put in your backpack. By the way, got any food in there?"** Bobby shook his head no.

"Well then, Bobby. Another thing to remember: Always take the proper food for the journey you're planning. **Take food that will last. Better yet, take food that never runs out. Ever.** You know what I'm talking about, don't you? It's the kind of food that got me through the World War Two army. **You need God's food.** Now that's food for your journey."

Stan had Bobby's full attention now. "So Bobby, I'm going to ask you again. Where are you going?"

* * * * * * * * *

I really like the way The Message Version of Scripture puts this:

"Jesus responded, "The real significance of that Scripture is not that Moses gave you bread from heaven but that my Father is right now offering you bread from heaven, the <u>real</u> bread. The Bread of God came down and is giving life to the world." They jumped at that: "Master, give us this bread, now and forever!"

Jesus said, "I am the Bread of Life. The person who aligns with me hungers no more and thirsts no more, ever. I have told you this explicitly because even though you have seen me in action, you don't really believe me. Every person the Father gives me eventually comes running to me. And once that person is with me, I hold on and don't let go."

What journey are you on? Where is your life headed – what is the goal of your life?

First we need to choose our destination, because until we do, it is impossible to know which way to head, identify the best paths leading towards that destination, and make necessary course corrections along the way. Without a destination in mind, we are truly lost in the wilderness of life.

Once we choose an ultimate destination, we can more **wisely choose our provisions** – the food for body, mind, and spirit which will get us to that destination. Jesus spoke, and speaks today, especially to the majority of us who so easily lose sight of our ultimate destination. Like young Bobby, we "pack our backpacks" with… whatever. We're going "out…wherever".

Be assured, once you "align with" Christ, accept His Bread of Life, that food will carry you through whatever... whenever, until you reach your final destination – eternal life with Him. As Jesus said, "*...once that person is with me, I hold on and don't let go.*"

* * * * * * * * *

Reflections...

What would you tell Bobby?

Each day the world seeks to "fill our backpacks" with...whatever. What spiritual practices do you (or will you try out) use to be sure you have the eternal provisions He provides you each day? Some examples are: prayer, Scripture reading and reflection, spiritual conversation and accountability with Christian friends.

Where is your life headed? If someone were to walk with you for a day, where would they say your life was headed?

What will you do to more and more closely "align your life with" Jesus as the Guide and Savior of your life? When will you begin?

28

Real Food

*"I am the bread of life. Your ancestors ate manna in the wilderness and they died. **This is the bread that comes down from heaven so that whoever eats from it will never die. I am the living bread that came down from heaven.***

***Whoever eats this bread will live forever,** and the bread that I will give for the life of the world is my flesh."* Then the Jews debated among themselves, asking, *"How can this man give us his flesh to eat?"*

*Jesus said to them, "I assure you, unless you eat the flesh of the Human One [1] and drink his blood, you have no life in you. Whoever eats my flesh and drinks my blood has eternal life, and I will raise them up at the last day. My flesh is true food and my blood is true drink. **Whoever eats my flesh and drinks my blood remains in me and I in them.** As the living Father sent me, and I live because of the Father, so whoever eats me lives because of me. This is the bread that came down from heaven. It isn't like the bread your ancestors ate, and then they died. **Whoever eats this bread will live forever."***
- John 6:48-58, Common English Bible

*"I am the Bread of Life. Your ancestors ate the manna bread in the desert and died. But now here is Bread that truly comes down out of heaven. Anyone eating this bread will not die, ever. **I am the Bread – living Bread! – who came down out of heaven. Anyone who eats this Bread will live – and forever!***

"The Bread that I present to the world so that it can eat and live is myself, this flesh-and-blood self." At this, the Jews started fighting among themselves: "How can this man serve up his flesh for a meal?"

*But Jesus didn't give an inch. "Only insofar as you eat and drink flesh and blood, the flesh and blood of the Son of Man, do you have life within you. The one who brings a hearty appetite to this eating and drinking has eternal life and will be fit and ready for the Final Day. My flesh is real food and my blood is real drink. **By eating my flesh and drinking my blood you enter into me and I into you.** In the same way that the fully alive Father sent me here and I live because of Him, so the one who makes a meal of me lives because of me. This is the Bread from heaven. Your ancestors ate bread and later died. **Whoever eats this Bread will live always."***
- John 6:48-58, The Message Version

* * * * * * * * * *

As they neared the long journey to their mission trip destination, Matt's stomach growled (for what felt like the zillionth time!). When would they get some food? The ten youth and three adult sponsors had left home yesterday early in the morning, and now it was, well, at least by home time, 8PM the next day. **The trip from Kansas City to Nairobi, Kenya seemed like it had taken forever!** All they'd had to eat was a long succession of peanuts and pretzels. Well, there was that weird sandwich thing they'd offered him—strange pasty stuff between what looked like really tough, chewy bread. Now he wished he'd at least tried it—maybe.

The team trooped off the airplane and into the Nairobi airport. Met by their mission hosts, soon they were on the way out of the big city toward their destination. The host driver turned to one of the adult sponsors. **"You hungry? As soon as we reach the village, we eat.** They been waiting for you a long time. Really excited, they are, yes!" *Ahhh, food!* Matt thought, as his stomach growled loudly enough for his best friend Nin to chuckle and elbow him in the ribs.

As they pulled into the village, Matt could smell wonderful things cooking. He looked around the center of the village and saw the cooking fires. Barbeque! He was so hungry, he almost didn't care what kind of meat it was (almost)! **If his stomach could, Matt knew it would reach out his throat and snag some of that wonderful-smelling meat right off the cooking fire!** Many came out to meet them, pouring out of the village huts and lean-to homes, laughing and cheering. Soon their gear was placed carefully in a hut that had been specially constructed for them. Matt just knew the food had to be next—yeah!

"Now we eat real food!", their host exclaimed happily. "Come this way!" *Wait a minute,* Matt thought, as they were led away from the food, *Whoa!* **What was this "real food"** *the host was talking about?* As they rounded the corner of a row of homes, a loud song burst out into the air. "Jesus is here!" was the only part He could pick out, but it did have an amazing beat, and soon they were all walking in rhythm to the singing. The people all rose from their seats on the ground and began clapping in time as they sang. *Was this the grace? Would they sing and then go eat, like the potlucks back home at church?*

Their host signaled them to sit, and the villagers all took seats as well. An old, wrinkled man walked in from the side. "That's our Christ-man, our pastor", the host whispered to them. **"He's here to give us real food before we go eat the temporary food."** *Temporary food?* Now Matt was interested. The pastor cleared his throat. **"We must share the Jesus-food, the forever-food, first** to remind us that God always stands ready to fill us with holiness, with grace, with wisdom, with strength to travel this life. This food will lead us to heaven! The food we share later will keep us for a time, but this food will keep us……(he paused expectantly). A mere heartbeat later, the entire village rang with one word: "FOREVER!" They shared prayer and Communion, and **somehow Matt didn't feel quite as hungry.** Oh, he ate his share of the wonderful evening meal, but the pastor's lesson of "real food" never left him.

* * * * * * * * *

Matt was transformed by his encounters and interactions. We live in a marketing-centered culture, which attempts (quite successfully overall) to define for us what we need, want, and pay attention to. Since the capacity of our attention is finite and limited, we allow these cultural forces to define such basic things as "food". **What is "food"?** Is some food more desirable than others? Why is this?

Scripture challenges us to take in ("eat") Jesus. As we mature in faith and discipleship, we should be more full of the essence of Jesus. We take in His body, and we become an integral part of His Body on earth. We take in his essence (seen in biblical times as blood), and His presence is what keeps us vibrantly alive. **The presence of Christ pumps and flows through us as we live, grow, and serve as His disciples! What could be more "real" than that?**

* * * * * * * * *

Reflections...

What is your "real food"?

How do you direct your heart to feast on the presence of Christ each day?

How do you reach out to God for, as some folks say, "a double dose of the Holy Ghost"?

How are you looking for the new spiritual food God is presenting in your life as God creates you anew each day?

I pray that you will experience much *real food* today – and every day!

29

The Power of Holy Company

He said these things while he was teaching in the synagogue at Capernaum. When many of his disciples heard it, they said, "This teaching is difficult; who can accept it?"

But Jesus, being aware that his disciples were complaining about it, said to them, "Does this offend you? Then what if you were to see the Son of Man ascending to where he was before? **It is the spirit that gives life;** *the flesh is useless.* **The words that I have spoken to you are spirit and life.**

But among you there are some who do not believe." For Jesus knew from the first who were the ones that did not believe, and who was the one that would betray him. And he said, "For this reason I have told you that no one can come to me unless it is granted by the Father."

Because of this many of his disciples turned back and no longer went about with him. So Jesus asked the twelve, "Do you also wish to go away?" Simon Peter answered him, "Lord, to whom can we go? You have the words of eternal life. *We have come to believe and know that you are the Holy One of God."*

Jesus answered them, "Did I not choose you, the twelve? Yet one of you is a devil." He was speaking of Judas son of Simon Iscariot, for he, though one of the twelve, was going to betray him.

- John 6:59-71, New Revised Standard Version

Jesus was teaching in a synagogue in Capernaum when He said these things. Many of Jesus' Disciples heard Him and said, "This is too hard for anyone to understand."

Jesus knew that His disciples were grumbling. So He asked, "Does this bother you? What if you should see the Son of Man go up to heaven where He came from? **The Spirit is the one who gives life!** *Human strength can do nothing.* **The words that I have spoken to you are from that life-giving Spirit.**

"But some of you refuse to have faith in me." Jesus said this, because from the beginning He knew who would have faith in Him. He also knew which one would betray Him. The Jesus said, "You cannot come to me, unless the Father makes you want to come. That is why I have told these things to all of you."

Because of what Jesus said, many of his disciples turned their backs on Him and stopped following Him. Jesus then asked His twelve disciples if they were going to leave Him. Simon Peter answered, "Lord, there is no one else that we can go to! Your words give eternal life. *We have faith in You, and we are sure that You are God's Holy One."*

Jesus told His disciples, "I chose all twelve of you, but one of you is a demon!" Jesus was talking about Judas, the son of Simon Iscariot. He would later betray Jesus, even though he was one of the twelve disciples.

- John 6:59-71, Contemporary English Version

* * * * * * * * *

The awful discovery hit him as he was unpacking the mission team's van. His voice loud enough to carry a city block, he yelled (more at himself than anyone else), **"Oh NO! I forgot the big box of tools – how are we going to build anything now?"**

Matt surely was not living up to the nickname the youth on the mission trip had given him - the "coordinator of materials procurement". Food and eating supplies? Check. Extra sleeping gear, first aid, bathroom supplies? Check. Tools to accomplish the mission of repairing, painting, etc., etc.? Oops.

Matt was so shocked at the discovery that he didn't realize just how far his voice had carried. Several of the youth came running out of the old shuttered church that would serve as their "home base" during the two-week mission project. The thirty-two youth and five sponsors were to complete repairs, paint, and re-landscape the small neighborhood church. In addition, they were scheduled to assist three of the elderly neighbors prepare their homes to be sold by cleaning, painting, completing minor repairs, and doing landscaping chores.

Darla, one of the youth, was the first of the group who came running to reach the van where Matt was still standing, hand on his head in disbelief that he could have overlooked something as vital as the tools. **"Great, Matt. So how are we going to fix anything without any tools? Just great."** She reached out and laid a hand on Matt's shoulder. "OK, you know what we need to do, right?   **It's like you always say – let's brainstorm with God!"**

Devon, another youth, wasn't so sure. "Come ON….look around you. Really? Where we gonna find tools…in this mess? I brought some games. **Maybe we just hang out and play games**….or something…"

Shaniqua shook her head. **"What are we going to tell these people – that we just gave UP? Seriously? I don't THINK so!"**

Devon looked at Shaniqua like she was the latest insane person he'd met. **"Yeah, right, like maybe God has some tools for us?"**

By now, a group of the mission team were gathered around the back of the van. They were so focused on the now-empty van that they **hadn't noticed the small boy on the bike who'd stopped to see what all the fuss was. "S'cuse me? Hey, mister? Hello?"** Darla was the first to notice him. Cute kid. Looked about the same age as her little cousin back home. "Hey there. I'm Darla. What's your name?"

"Well….my grandma said never, ever to tell strangers my name, and you look…well….strange in <u>this</u> neighborhood anyway. But **I can take you to my house, and my grandpa's got tools.** That's what you need, right? Tools? Grandpa, he doesn't get out of bed much any more, but **I heard you talkin' about God, and my grandma does that too. Maybe she can help you with that, that 'stormin' God thing you were talkin' about."**

That's how it started. "Grandma Ruthie", as the neighborhood called her, was amazing. She began calling people. Matt lost count of the number of phone calls she made. This lady seemed to know everyone! Each call she made began the same way: "Ruth calling….how you doin'? **We got some holy company over here at the old church, and our holy company needs help. You know what that means, don't you. God's callin', and we've got to answer. Got any tools?"**

Grandma Ruth turned with a big smile as Shaniqua brought her a cool glass of water. "Girl, you remember one thing: **Holy Company, now that's a powerful thing. Look for it, grow it, count on it. Got it?"** Shaniqua nodded. **"Yes, ma'am. I got it."**

And they all "got it". Tools of all shapes and sizes seemed to pour out of the neighborhood to the little church. They even had to make one of the church classrooms into their mission team's "tool depot". Two weeks later the little church held its first worship service in twenty years, and it was standing room only! The homes the team had worked on were almost unrecognizable – they looked marvelous!

As Grandma Ruth stood to share the worship message, her first words brought tears to many of those gathered: "God is in the house!", she exclaimed. **"Never, ever, never doubt the power of Holy Company!"**

* * * * * * * * * *

Sometimes the task ahead of us seems so big, and many times we just don't think we have the tools (abilities, resources,…) to accomplish it. In the midst of our struggles, we lose sight of the amazing power of our "Holy Company" - the Spirit who gives us life, and the Word made flesh – Jesus the Christ – in our midst.

Like young Devon, **we are often tempted to give up**. In fact, sometimes we do. We forget that above all, the Spirit gives life that cannot be defeated. **In the Holy Company of Christ**, living and serving as part of the Body of Christ, our life's toolbox will be filled with all that is necessary. That is serious, eternal power!

* * * * * * * * * *

Reflections...

Who did you most identify with in the story? Why do you think that is?

That small neighborhood church became the neighborhood "Mission Station". Within a year, it was home to a counseling and health clinic, an after school program, and a food pantry. Pictures of that youth mission team and a collection of crosses made during their time there adorn the entry walls of the church. A beautiful carved sign displays the new name of the sanctuary: "God's Tool Depot". **Why do you think this name is so important to them?**

Do you keep "Holy Company" in your life? If so, what difference <u>does</u> it make? If not, what difference do you think it <u>could</u> make?

30

Seriously?

After this, Jesus traveled around Galilee. He wanted to stay out of Judea, where the Jewish leaders were plotting his death. But soon it was time for the Jewish Festival of Shelters,and Jesus' brothers said to him, "Leave here and go to Judea, where your followers can see your miracles!

You can't become famous if you hide like this! **If you can do such wonderful things, show yourself to the world!"** *For even his brothers didn't believe in him.*

Jesus replied, **"Now is not the right time for me to go, but you can go anytime.** *The world can't hate you, but it does hate me because I accuse it of doing evil. You go on. I'm not going to this festival, because my time has not yet come." After saying these things, Jesus remained in Galilee. But after his brothers left for the festival, Jesus also went, though secretly, staying out of public view. The Jewish leaders tried to find him at the festival and kept asking if anyone had seen him.*

There was a lot of grumbling about him among the crowds. Some argued, "He's a good man," but others said, "He's nothing but a fraud who deceives the people." But no one had the courage to speak favorably about him in public, for they were afraid of getting in trouble with the Jewish leaders. - *John 7:1-13, New Living Translation*

Later Jesus was going about His business in Galilee. He didn't want to travel in Judea because the Jews there were looking for a chance to kill Him. It was near the time of Tabernacles, a feast observed annually by the Jews.

His brothers said, "Why don't you leave here and go up to the Feast so your disciples can get a good look at the works you do? No one who intends to be publicly known does everything behind the scenes. **If you're serious about what you are doing,** *come out in the open and show the world." His brothers were pushing him like this because they didn't believe in him either.*

Jesus came back at them, "Don't crowd me. **This isn't my time. It's your time – it's _always_ your time; you have nothing to lose.** *The world has nothing against you, but it's up in arms against me. It's against me because I expose evil behind its pretensions. You go ahead, go up to the Feast. Don't wait for me. I'm not ready. It's not the right time for me."*

He said this and stayed on in Galilee. But later, after his family had gone up to the Feast, he also went. But he kept out of the way, careful not to draw attention to himself. The Jews were already out looking for him, asking around, "Where is that man?"

There was a lot of contentious talk about him circulating through the crowds. Some were saying, "He's a good man." But others said, "Not so. He's selling snake oil." This kind of talk went on in guarded whispers because of the intimidating Jewish leaders. - *John 7:1-13, The Message Version*

* * * * * * * * * *

"Are you the...chemist...we've been waiting for?" Ben was a chemist, and he was here to help with a clean water filtration project, but Ben was also...a Christian missionary. His Pakistani hosts had given him careful instructions. Over and over, they told him, "You are a chemist. **If you want to live to return home, you are a chemist."**

So any time an official (or anyone else for that matter) asked him who he was, why he was traveling to Pakistan, anything...Ben always answered: "I am a chemist...here to help with clean water." That much was certainly true, but Ben had an additional purpose. **He also hoped to share the Living Water of Christ with those he would meet.**

Given these very definite (and determined) traveling instructions, **Ben was quite surprised at his welcome the next Sunday evening as he was welcomed to the small basement church.** He had never experienced being part of a church so persecuted it had to meet in secret, continually changing its worship time and place. He quickly realized that **his hosts had not exaggerated the danger** he faced as a Christian here.

Ben was more than surprised. He was shocked by the words one elder spoke to him as worship began: "We are so happy you are here. **Now you can go out and show the people around here how wonderful Jesus is!"** *Seriously? Are these people crazy? Chemist. Water. Are they crazy? Seriously?*

Ben soon realized his thoughts must be showing on his face. **"Why me?"** he asked them. "Well," they answered, **"Like the Book says, nobody should do anything in secret if they want people to know. So you should go show them Jesus!"**

Ben took a deep breath. In addition to preparing and gathering knowledge and resources to address the very real and urgent need for his expertise in water filtration, Ben had spent much time in prayer as he prepared for this trip. **"This is not my time and place. It is yours. I am here to help you. Here in this place, your time is always here."**

"Seriously?" they asked. Ben's answer? **"Yes, seriously. God is serious with you."** This became his answer so often that soon he overheard them saying it to one another when worry or fear threatened to overtake them.

So began an amazing four months in Pakistan. Ben met many interesting people as he helped the people design and build water filtration and purification devices and systems. What a difference clean, safe water made! He also coached and taught in the "underground" Christian church, which soon bore the name that loosely translated as **"Church of the Ever-Clean Water".**

Ben was even more amazed at the strength of the Christian community there. He knew he was being observed closely and diligently by those whom he had learned wouldn't hesitate to harm (or even kill) him if they knew he was there for more than earthly water purposes. But it seemed the more persecuted they felt, the more they had to change worship times and places, the stronger they became.

Oh, and their new "code word" for believers? It was...."Seriously?"

* * * * * * * * * *

How serious are you about connecting – and living out – the strength your relationship with Christ as His disciple gives you? **Often we expect someone else** to act out our discipleship for us. In other words, we choose them as our "disciple-proxies". Perhaps it's a friend, parent or grandparent, or our pastor.

Seriously? It would do us well to remember: This is our time. Each one of us. Seriously. Yes, God is indeed serious with us. So serious God sent, sacrificed, and resurrected His Son to demonstrate it – seriously.

* * * * * * * * *

Reflections...

Why do you think people choose "proxy-disciples"?

God is serious about you. What does this statement mean to you?

How serious are you about your discipleship to Christ? What evidence shows your seriousness?

31

Who Says?

About the middle of the festival Jesus went up into the temple and began to teach. The Jews were astonished at it, saying, **"How does this man have such learning,** *when he has never been taught?"*

Then Jesus answered them, "My teaching is not mine but his who sent me. Anyone who resolves to do the will of God will know whether the teaching is from God or whether I am speaking on my own. **Those who speak on their own seek their own glory; but the one who seeks the glory of him who sent him is true, and there is nothing false in him.**

"Did not Moses give you the law? Yet none of you keeps the law. Why are you looking for an opportunity to kill me?" The crowd answered, "You have a demon! Who is trying to kill you?"

Jesus answered them, "I performed one work, and all of you are astonished. Moses gave you circumcision (it is, of course, not from Moses, but from the patriarchs), and you circumcise a man on the Sabbath. If a man receives circumcision on the Sabbath in order that the law of Moses may not be broken, are you angry with me because I healed a man's whole body on the Sabbath? **Do not judge by appearances, but judge with right judgment."**

- John 7:14-24, New Revised Standard Version

Halfway through the festival, Jesus went up to the temple and started to teach. Astonished, the Jewish leaders asked, "He's never been taught! How has he mastered the Law?"

Jesus responded, "My teaching isn't mine but comes from the one who sent me. Whoever wants to do God's will can tell whether my teaching is from God or whether I speak on my own. **Those who speak on their own seek glory for themselves. Those who seek the glory of him who sent me are people of truth; there's no falsehood in them.**

Didn't Moses give you the Law? Yet none of you keep the Law. Why do you want to kill me?" The crowd answered, "You have a demon. Who wants to kill you?"

Jesus replied, "I did one work, and you were all astonished. Because Moses gave you the commandment about circumcision (although it wasn't Moses but the patriarchs), you circumcise a man on the Sabbath. If a man can be circumcised on the Sabbath without breaking Moses' Law, why are you angry with me because I made an entire man well on the Sabbath? **Don't judge according to appearances. Judge with right judgment."**

- John 7:14-24, Common English Bible

* * * * * * * * * *

Rita was still shaking as Toby, the new boy in her class, walked away. As soon as her friends started gathering around her, it seemed he realized that he was outnumbered. In the three weeks since Toby had moved into the neighborhood – and been assigned the desk next to Rita in Mrs. Wallis's fourth grade class – **he had pushed her down (or tried to) almost every day he could get close enough to her on the school playground.**

Her friends had all kinds of advice:

"You shoulda just hit him…hard!"

"Yeah, real hard…he's mean."

"Yeah, why dincha? He's meaner than mean!"

They all looked expectantly at Rita for an explanation. They were more than puzzled that Rita, who was at least four inched taller and ten pounds heavier than Toby, hadn't just, as one put it so descriptively, "beat him up and get it over with". **Every time they asked her why not, Rita would answer, "It's not right. I can't do that."**

And every time Rita told them that hurting Toby wasn't right, **their answer was the same: "Who says?"**

Today, however, Rita decided to answer her friends. **"God says. And it's not about me, either."**

Rita's friend Violet shot back, "You're the one getting shoved around. If it's not about you, then who IS it about? Whack him good, that's what I say!" Her three other friends nodded in agreement.

Rita decided to explain her decision. "My new basketball coach told us something when we first started the season this year. She said, **'People will know what team you're on by the way you play, and the way you treat other people, whether you win or lose, but especially when you lose.'** I don't know what Toby's problem is, but I know whose team I'm on. God's team. And people on that team don't beat people up."

As Rita opened her front door that day, she was surprised (shocked, really) to see **Toby sitting at their dining room table drinking lemonade with her mom.** "Honey, I'm so glad you're home. Toby here came over, and we've been talking…"

And….., thought Rita as she let her backpack slide to the floor. Now what….

Toby started to speak, but no words came out. Rita's mom explained. "Honey, I think what Toby wants to say is that…." Toby found his voice. "I didn't go home when you thought I did. I snuck around behind the bleachers so I could hear what you and your friends were saying. I spied on you. **So why didn't you hit me? Really. Why?"**

Rita was really tired of being asked this question! "It's just not right. That's why. **I get to pick what team I'm on, and the team I'm on, we don't beat people up."**

Now Toby looked confused. "I thought I heard something about a team, but it sounded weird. **Whose team?"**

Rita took a deep breath, and as her mom nodded in support, she said, **"God's team.** I'm on God's team. The coach is Jesus, and beating people up, well, that's not in His game plan."

* * * * * * * * *

"Those who speak on their own seek glory for themselves. Those who seek the glory of him who sent me are people of truth; there's no falsehood in them."

No one was more surprised than Rita when **Toby knocked on their door Sunday morning asking if he could come with them to church.** Having never been in a church (his family had never been), **he wanted to meet "Coach Jesus" and learn more about this "God's team".** And he did. Soon Toby brought his younger brother Mack along to join the new team. When Rita's parents learned that Toby and Mack were being raised by their seventeen year old big brother, they went into action. Rita's dad came alongside seventeen year old Eddie and began "guys' Saturdays", spending hours with the boys mentoring and having fun together.

"Don't judge according to appearances. Judge with right judgment."

Six months later, Rita's parents applied to adopt all three boys. Eddie was able to begin college the next fall, and both Toby and Mack just glowed with happiness now that they had a new family and a new team – God's team.

* * * * * * * * *

Reflections...

Think about Rita's response: "Who says?" "God says. And it's not about me, either. My new basketball coach told us …'People will know what team you're on by the way you play, and the way you treat other people, whether you win or lose, but especially when you lose.' I don't know what Toby's problem is, but **I know whose team I'm on. God's team.** And people on that team don't beat people up."

After being pushed down twice, Rita took what she called "evasive action" whenever Toby came near. She moved toward other people, either friends or adults. She never hit him, even though she was bigger and could have hurt him. **Where do you think Rita got the strength to respond to Toby's bullying the way she did?**

Reflections (continued)

It's not just children who face these kinds of challenges. Adults often face situations of bullying (emotional, physical, even spiritual). Sometimes we're the friends of the one being challenged. **If Rita were an adult who was being bullied in some way, how would you encourage her?**

If Toby were an adult, and your friend, how would you encourage him?

32

In the Open

Some of the people from Jerusalem were saying, **"Isn't this the man they want to kill? Yet here he is, speaking for everyone to hear. And no one is arguing with him. Do you suppose the authorities know he is the Messiah?** *But how could that be? No one knows where the Messiah will come from, but we know where this man comes from."*

As Jesus was teaching in the Temple, he shouted, *"Do you really think you know me and where I came from? I didn't come on my own!* **The one who sent me is truthful, and you don't know him.** *But I know the one who sent me, because I came from him."*

Some of the people wanted to arrest Jesus right then. But no one even laid a hand on him, because his time had not yet come. A lot of people in the crowd put their faith in him and said, "When the Messiah comes, he surely won't perform more miracles than this man has done!"

When the Pharisees heard the crowd arguing about Jesus, they got together with the chief priests and sent some Temple police to arrest him. But Jesus told them, "I will be with you a little while longer, and then I will return to the one who sent me. You will look for me, but you won't find me. You cannot go where I am going."

The people asked each other, **"Where can he go to keep us from finding him?** *Is he going to some foreign country where our people live? Is he going there to teach the Greeks? What did he mean by saying that we will look for him, but won't find him? Why can't we go where he is going?"* — John 7:25-36, Contemporary English Version

That's when some of the people of Jerusalem said, **"Isn't this the one they were out to kill? And here he is out in the open saying whatever he pleases, and no one is stopping him. Could it be that the rulers know that he is, in fact, the Messiah?** *And yet we know where this man comes from. The Messiah is going to come out of nowhere. Nobody is going to know where he comes from."*

That provoked Jesus, who was teaching in the Temple, to cry out, *"Yes, you think you know me and where I'm from. I didn't set myself up in business.* **My true origin is in the One who sent me, and you don't know him at all.** *I come from him — that's how I know him. He sent me here."*

They were looking for a way to arrest him, but not a hand was laid on him because it wasn't yet God's time. Many from the crowd committed themselves in faith to him, saying, "Will the Messiah, when he comes, provide better or more convincing evidence than this?

The Pharisees, alarmed at this seditious undertow going through the crowd, teamed up with the high priests and sent their police to arrest him. Jesus rebuffed them: "I am with you only a short time. Then I go on to the One who sent me. You will look for me, but you won't find me. Where I am, you can't come."

*The Jews put their heads together. "**Where do you think he is going that we won't be able to find him?** Do you think he is about to travel to the Greek world to teach the Jews? What is he talking about anyway: 'You will look for me, but you won't find me,' and 'Where I am, you can't come'?"* - John 7:25-36, The Message Version

* * * * * * * * *

"My neighbor told me you're the people who bring the food, and you come from that church down on the corner; but we know that church, and....well,...number one – never knew they did that sort of thing, and number two – shhhhh! Better be quiet about it if it is, because this **place gets government grants, and you know how THEY are!"**

The woman really was trying to be helpful...I think. We were in fact from "that church down on the corner". For the past several months, we'd been providing a monthly roomful of free rummage, including many brand new items much needed by the residents of the low-income apartment complex. In addition, we provided a plentiful evening meal and sent leftovers home with residents. We placed invitations to worship, as well as programs and activities of our congregation, in rummage shopping bags and on the food tables.

Later, as we were setting up the rummage tables, one of the apartment complex administrators came by and stopped one of our volunteers. **"We need to downplay the church thing.** We don't want to mess up any of our funding, so could you just not put anything out that talks about the church? That way, nobody will know the food and stuff is connected to the church."

He didn't even hesitate. **"Don't think that'll work for us, ma'am. See, I don't think our faith should be hidden.** Jesus was out there in the open, even when they were plotting and planning to do him in. If we bring this food and these gifts, and minister with these great people because we follow Him, then how can we hide the same kind of thing He did in the open? I mean, **He didn't hide from the government when He healed people's lives, did he?"**

So began the challenge. **In the open? Or not?** Those who served in the church's "Neighbor Care" team decided they would follow the "in the open" example of Jesus. They even researched and planned an alternate site just in case the apartment complex asked them to leave.

As the residents gathered that evening for food and rummage, the woman who had approached me earlier in the afternoon found me again. "You ARE from that church! I heard they tried to get you to hide all your church stuff. Don't do it! **I know for a fact that you guys are the only picture of a caring church that a lot of these people ever see, so please don't hide the church stuff."**

We chose "in the open". The seeds of faith and grace which were planted, nourished, and grown through that ministry were truly amazing. The results of those planted seeds went places we'll never know (but God surely does).

* * * * * * * * *

Jesus didn't hide who He was. In fact, he raised His voice to be sure they heard! He shouted: *"Yes, you think you know me and where I'm from. I didn't set myself up in business. **My true origin is in the One who sent me, and you don't know him at all.** I come from him – that's how I know him. He sent me here."* (vv. 28-29)

Then, upon being challenged once more by the governing powers (chief priests and Pharisees), He asserts His identity again, even more clearly (just in case it wasn't clear enough the last time): *"I will be with you a little while longer, and then I will return to the one who sent me. You will look for me, but you won't find me. You cannot go where I am going."* (vv. 33-34)

It is so tempting, and sometimes seems SO much easier, to hide our discipleship to Christ. Yet if we truly follow His example, we will seek opportunities to act out our discipleship, wherever life takes us, in any and all situations we find ourselves in.

* * * * * * * * *

Reflections...

What was your first reaction as you read this true story? Why do you think you reacted that way?

Why do you think people mask their identity as followers, disciples of Christ?

How would your life be different if your discipleship was more "in the open"?

33

Carried Away – By What?

On the last day of the festival, the great day, while Jesus was standing there, he cried out, "Let anyone who is thirsty come to me, and let the one who believes in me drink. As the scripture has said, **'Out of the believer's heart shall flow rivers of living water.'"** *Now he said this about the Spirit, which believers in him were to receive; for as yet there was no Spirit, because Jesus was not yet glorified.*

When they heard these words, some in the crowd said, "This is really the prophet." **Others said, "This is the Messiah."** *But some asked, "Surely the Messiah does not come from Galilee, does he? Has not the scripture said that the Messiah is descended from David and comes from Bethlehem, the village where David lived?"*

So there was a division in the crowd because of him. *Some of them wanted to arrest him, but no one laid hands on him. Then the temple police went back to the chief priests and Pharisees, who asked them, "Why did you not arrest him?" The police answered,* **"Never has anyone spoken like this!"**

Then the Pharisees replied, "Surely you have not been deceived too, have you? Has any one of the authorities or of the Pharisees believed in him? But this crowd, which does not know the law-- they are accursed."
                                                    - John 7:37-49, New Revised Standard Version

On the last day, the climax of the festival, Jesus stood and shouted to the crowds, "Anyone who is thirsty may come to me! Anyone who believes in me may come and drink! For the Scriptures declare, **'Rivers of living water will flow from his heart.'** *" (When he said "living water," he was speaking of the Spirit, who would be given to everyone believing in him. But the Spirit had not yet been given, because Jesus had not yet entered into his glory.)*

When the crowds heard him say this, some of them declared, "Surely this man is the Prophet we've been expecting." **Others said, "He is the Messiah."** *Still others said,* **"But he can't be!** *Will the Messiah come from Galilee? For the Scriptures clearly state that the Messiah will be born of the royal line of David, in Bethlehem, the village where King David was born."*

So the crowd was divided about him. Some even wanted him arrested, but no one laid a hand on him. When the Temple guards returned without having arrested Jesus, the leading priests and Pharisees demanded, "Why didn't you bring him in?" **"We have never heard anyone speak like this!"** *the guards responded.*

"Have you been led astray, too?" *the Pharisees mocked.* **"Is there a single one of us rulers or Pharisees who believes in him? This foolish crowd follows him, but they are ignorant of the law. God's curse is on them!"**
                                                    - John 7:37-49, New Living Translation

* * * * * * * * *

107

The canoe trip down the lazy river was great! But much to his surprise, as Jack's canoe rounded a bend, the river forked in front of him. Left? Right? Which one? Before he could even gather his thoughts enough to make an informed decision, his canoe (and the river) made the decision for him.

Swoosh! Jack figured he'd remember the sound of the river sucking him into the current as long as he lived. Into the left fork he went...**right into some really nasty rapids!** Eyes wide open in shock, the sound of his screams swallowed up in the roar of the fast-moving, foam-topped rapids, Jack prayed like never before in his life. He did his best to push off the rocks with his canoe paddle, one rock, one second, one prayer at a time.

Jack was so busy that he almost (almost) didn't notice the small drop-off looming ahead, until.....over he went. Thankfully Jack had time (and a paddle left) to turn his canoe for the best angle. He was much more than thankful that, (1) the drop-off wasn't as big as it looked at first; and (2) he stayed upright and in one piece as he went over.

Jack was amazed as he looked around him at the calm, beautiful water. Could it be that just moments ago he'd been afraid for his life as he fought the crazy, wild rapids of this same river?

As he paddled farther into the small, peaceful river cove, **Jack thought about his life.** He realized there was very little about the last ten years he could remember. Caught up in fourteen hour days, and at least eight months of every year on the road, he almost turned down his pastor's gift – a canoe and a week in a cabin in the woods. Jack had always wanted a canoe (when he retired – whenever that was), so when Pastor Joe said he could <u>have</u> one <u>now</u>, he couldn't turn it down. "But, Jack," Pastor Joe had stopped him in his excitement, "There's a condition..." *Uh oh, now what?* Jack remembered thinking. "You'll have to earn the canoe..." *Uh huh, keep talking....what's the catch...* Joe smiled. "You'll earn it by keeping an eye on my cabin for a week. That'd be seven days. Do that, and the canoe's yours to keep. By the way, the cabin is right on the river, and that's where your new canoe is."

As Jack sat in the calm water in his new canoe, he realized the wisdom of his pastor. Joe knew this river like the back of his hand, and Jack faintly remembered Joe telling him he'd find real living water on that river. **Pastor Joe warned him to watch out for the rapids – the ones in the river, and the ones threatening him in his life.** Jack had nodded and smiled, not really listening – until now.

The next day, Jack took the same course down the river. He was more careful this time, and he was surprised to find out how many of the signs of impending rapids he'd missed the day before. How could he have missed all those signs? This time, he took the right fork of the river. It went down a gentle curved slope, emptying into the same beautiful cove he'd ended up in before.

On that river (which he nicknamed "living water river"), **Jack realized his whole life had been swept away into some dangerous and fast-moving currents.** He'd lost sight of his faith, his family, and his friends. He had let unhealthy habits and life-destroying priorities literally sweep him away. **God was offering him a return to the Living Water of Christ.**

Jack knew that when he returned to his work world, nothing would have changed much. But Jack had changed. He knew there would be challenges; the rapids of life would still be there, threatening to pull him under. **But now Jack was stronger. He had Living Water, and nothing was going to take that away from him. Nothing.**

* * * * * * * * *

Those who heard Jesus in the Temple that day had a life-changing choice: **accept the living water (Jesus really was the Messiah), or keep on going the way they were, totally missing the signs which led to Christ.** The Pharisees (totally absorbed in the "rules of the river") completely missed the signs, so much that even when they clearly showed Jesus to be the Christ, the Messiah, they pointedly chose not to see, not to believe. Worse, they also used every persuasive tool they could to dissuade anyone else from accepting the living water of Christ, saying: *"Is there a single one of us rulers or Pharisees who believes in him? This foolish crowd follows him, but they are ignorant of the law. God's curse is on them!"* (v. 49)

Things aren't so different today. There are forces in the world which deny the presence and power of Christ's offer of living water. **Like Jack, we too are lured "down the river"** toward fast-moving, dangerous rapids which threaten to destroy our lives. Like Jack, if we look, we will see Christ steadfastly continuing to offer us His living water. Christ offers us direction to the calm, strengthening and refreshing coves in the river of life.

The question is: **Who (or what) will we let carry us away on the river of our lives?**

* * * * * * * * *

Reflections...

What advice would you give Jack?

Think of a time in your life when you realized you were headed the wrong way. What was that like? Are you there now?

What resources are available to you which will help you identify the "signs of the river" in your life? Are you taking advantage of them, or are you allowing life to just sweep you along?

34

Taking Sides

Nicodemus, who had gone to Jesus before, and who was one of them, asked, "Our law does not judge people without first giving them a hearing to find out what they are doing, does it?" They replied, "Surely you are not also from Galilee, are you? Search and you will see that no prophet is to arise from Galilee."

Then each of them went home, while Jesus went to the Mount of Olives. Early in the morning he came again to the temple. All the people came to him and he sat down and began to teach them.

The scribes and the Pharisees brought a woman who had been caught in adultery; and making her stand before all of them, they said to him, "Teacher, this woman was caught in the very act of committing adultery. **Now in the law Moses commanded us to stone such women. Now what do you say?"** *They said this to test him, so that they might have some charge to bring against him.*

Jesus bent down and wrote with his finger on the ground. When they kept on questioning him, he straightened up and said to them, **"Let anyone among you who is without sin be the first to throw a stone at her."** *And once again he bent down and wrote on the ground. When they heard it, they went away, one by one, beginning with the elders; and Jesus was left alone with the woman standing before him.*

Jesus straightened up and said to her, "Woman, where are they? **Has no one condemned you?" She said, "No one, sir." And Jesus said, "Neither do I condemn you.** *Go your way, and from now on do not sin again."*
- John 7:50 - 8:11, New Revised Standard Version

Nicodemus, who was one of them and had come to Jesus earlier, said, "Our Law doesn't judge someone without first hearing him and learning what he is doing, does it?" They answered him, "You are not from Galilee too, are you? Look it up and you will see that the prophet doesn't come from Galilee."

They each went to their own homes, and Jesus went to the Mount of Olives. Early in the morning he returned to the temple. All the people gathered around him, and he sat down and taught them.

The legal experts and Pharisees brought a woman caught in adultery. Placing her in the center of the group, they said to Jesus, "Teacher, this woman was caught in the act of committing adultery. In the Law, **Moses commanded us to stone women like this. What do you say?"** *They said this to test him, because they wanted a reason to bring an accusation against him.*

Jesus bent down and wrote on the ground with his finger. They continued to question him, so he stood up and replied, **"Whoever hasn't sinned should throw the first stone."** *Bending down again, he wrote on the ground. Those who heard him went away, one by one, beginning with the elders.*

Finally, only Jesus and the woman were left in the middle of the crowd. Jesus stood up and said to her, "Woman, where are they? **Is there no one to condemn you?"** *She said, "No one, sir."* **Jesus said, "Neither do I condemn you.** *Go, and from now on, don't sin anymore."*   *- John 7:50 – 8:11, Common English Bible*

* * * * * * * * *

His brother didn't deserve a big birthday party with all the cake, friends, and presents – and Jerry knew it. The only problem was that this wasn't just any brother, it was his **twin** brother. They shared a birthday. Always had, always would. But that didn't mean they had to celebrate it the same. **It just wasn't fair, and he was going to let his mom know it.**

Jerry went out to his mom's "art studio" (garage). As he entered, mom was just putting a new piece of canvas on her painting easel. **Jerry loved to watch his mom paint.** His favorite moment was when he finally figured out just what mom was painting, when enough paint was on the canvas that he could be sure what it would be.

"Mom," he began, **"I wanted to ask you something about my birthday."** She immediately looked up, pausing in her choosing and arranging the charcoal pencils and paint she planned to use. "Son, don't you mean 'our birthday'? You and Jimmy have always shared your birthday together. You thinking maybe now you're going to be ten you want your own? Maybe then one of you could have a party Friday and the other Saturday – that it?"

"Well, sort of...", Jerry began. Mom started sketching, just a little. *What was she going to paint this time?* He wondered. She put down the pencil and picked up a brush. "Jerry, I know when something's bothering you. What is it?"

Jerry took a deep breath. "Well, mom...." All of a sudden, it all came out. **"You know Jimmy stole that stuff at the store, and he's flunking math and English, and he didn't do any of his chores, and...."**

Mom put the brush down. Jerry looked at the canvas, trying to figure out what the picture could be.... "So, **I'm hearing that you don't think he deserves a birthday, is that it? Or maybe it's that you don't want to share your day with him because you've judged him a thief, lazy, and a sneaky liar – that about cover it?"** Now Jerry knew his mom; he knew when he was on shaky ground – and this was it.

Mom picked up the brush again and began to paint. Jerry knew better than to interrupt her now, so he sat, waiting and watching her paint. He could pick out a pile of rocks in her painting. Hmmm... She picked up another brush, more colors, and went back to work. **As he watched, a figure appeared,** bent over the rock pile as if trying to choose the best rock. Then once more she put down the brush and chose another, along with other colors. Soon the empty center of the canvas contained the image of a pit; soon after that the figure of a person huddled down in that pit.

"Jerry, do you know what's missing from this picture?" she asked him. He thought, and looked, and shrugged. "Nope" was his answer. "Watch" was her only response as **she added another figure.** As the figure of Jesus appeared in his mom's picture, and Jesus' hand held a stick, and that stick was drawing in the sand, Jerry finally got it. Mom looked up, smiling at him. "Son, I **do** love you. And I love your brother too. **I'm really glad neither of you are perfect, because that means you both need Jesus, just like the rest of us, right?"** And all he could do was nod through his suddenly too-wet eyes.

I have what I call a "first stone" on my desk. On one side, it simply says "first"; on the other, "John 8:7". It reminds me that I need to think before I judge another. It reminds me that Jesus judges with grace, with love. It's His reminder of who I am, and Who I follow...

* * * * * * * * * *

We often want to position ourselves on one "side" or another: completely guilty...or completely innocent. We choose sides, and then we tend to define ourselves by what side we place ourselves on. We say to ourselves (maybe others as well), "I'm not at fault here. It's not my fault." Other times our lines might be, "Wow, did I mess up. I've had it now; can't possibly fix this..."

Most times (OK, almost all the time), **the total truth of where we stand in life is somewhere in between.** Our life stories, and thus our identity before God and one another, is a combination of victories and failures, good choices and bad, sure steps and mis-steps.

Like Jerry, when we are tempted to condemn another, we need to step back and ask ourselves, "Is this my job?" Notice that his mother didn't say his brother Jimmy was right, or that his behavior was good. She invited Jerry into the story of Jesus' teaching about judging one another. **She invited him to see a whole other "side" he hadn't noticed – God's side.**

The truth is, none of us can possibly be totally on "God's side". Our behavior gives us away – we are imperfect, and our actions demonstrate that all too clearly. We are the forgiven and those in the process of being forgiven. We are the forgiving - and those in the process <u>of</u> forgiving others.

Only God can be God. We are called to treat one another as those created in the image of God, as precious children for whom God sacrificed His Son to redeem and reconcile. Each time we follow Christ in this way, we draw closer to the side of God.

* * * * * * * * * *

Reflections...

What do you think Jerry's mother was trying to teach him?

Reflections (continued)

When you find yourself in a position like young Jerry, what resources do you have which help you? How do you use them?

Think of a situation in your life (or perhaps your community, nation, or world) in which there is a compulsion toward "side-taking". To the best of your ability (none of us is God) how would you describe the "God-side" of that situation?

35

Reliable Evidence

*Once again Jesus spoke to the people. This time he said, "**I am the light of the world! Follow me, and you won't be walking in the dark. You will have the light that gives life.**"*

The Pharisees objected, "You are the only one speaking for yourself, and what you say isn't true!"

*Jesus replied, "Even if I do speak for myself, what I say is true! I know where I came from and where I am going. But you don't know where I am from or where I am going. **You judge in the same way that everyone else does, but I don't judge anyone. If I did judge, I would judge fairly, because I would not be doing it alone.** The Father who sent me is here with me. Your Law requires two witnesses to prove that something is true. I am one of my witnesses, and the Father who sent me is the other one.*

"Where is your Father?" they asked.

*"**You don't know me or my Father!**" Jesus answered. "**If you knew me, you would know my Father.**"*

Jesus said this while he was still teaching in the place where the temple treasures were stored. But no one arrested him, because his time had not yet come.   *- John 8:12-20, Contemporary English Version*

*Jesus once again addressed them: "**I am the world's Light. No one who follows me stumbles around in the darkness. I provide plenty of light to live in.**"*

The Pharisees objected, "All we have is your word on this. We need more than this to go on."

*Jesus replied, "You're right that you only have my word. But you can depend on it being true. I know where I've come from and where I go next. You don't know where I'm from or where I'm headed. **You decide according to what you can see and touch. I don't make judgments like that. But even if I did, my judgment would be true because I wouldn't make it out of the narrowness of my experience** but in the largeness of the One who sent me, the Father. That fulfills the conditions set down in God's Law: that you can count on the testimony of two witnesses. And that is what you have: You have my word and you have the word of the Father who sent me."*

They said, "Where is this so-called Father of yours?"

*Jesus said, "**You're looking right at me and you don't see me. How do you expect to see the Father? If you knew me, you would at the same time know the Father.**"*

He gave this speech in the Treasury while teaching in the Temple. No one arrested him because his time wasn't yet up.   *- John 8:11-20, The Message Version*

* * * * * * * * *

Jury duty. Those two words stir a variety of reactions. Most value a justice system which includes decisions made by a group of one's peers. They just aren't thrilled to be called to serve as one of those peers sitting in judgment. Some chafe at the time spent sitting (often all day) waiting to see if their juror services will be needed. Others relish a day of reading a favorite book, catching up with letter writing, or meeting new people.

I observed all these possibilities as I responded to a call to jury duty. I met interesting people as I relaxed in the central potential juror area with a mystery novel which I hadn't had time to finish reading in the last month. **Many conversations I overheard centered on what people could be doing if it didn't take so much time to see if they were needed for jury duty.**

As time went by and groups of potential jurors were called, the population of the waiting area shrank. As the latest group to be called was led out of the central area, a man sitting next to me turned to me. "I wonder if we're going to get called at all. You know, it's not the time I mind. **It's just,... I don't know what I'd do if I ever actually got put on a jury."**

Thinking he was referring perhaps to time spent away from work and/or family, I began to respond with something like, "Yeah, it can take days..." but stopped when he shook his head 'no'.

"No, it's not the time I'd mind. Not at all. It's just, well...**It's so hard to know what's really true.** I mean, they say different things. **How do you decide for sure who's telling the absolute truth, and which evidence is really reliable?** Somebody's life is on the line, and **I'm afraid I wouldn't be able to tell which evidence was completely reliable."**

✳ ✳ ✳ ✳ ✳ ✳ ✳ ✳ ✳ ✳

It wasn't just the Pharisees who yearned for absolutely, 100% reliable evidence that Jesus was who He said he was. **It wasn't only the disciples** who kept asking Jesus to demonstrate undeniable, absolutely reliable evidence of His Messiahship.

How often do <u>we</u> yearn for "reliable evidence" that Christ is present with us in the midst of our current struggles and triumphs (and everything in between)? Prayers such as "God, please be with us...." or "Lord, come into this place..." demonstrate our yearning for reliable evidence of God's presence.

God is present. In every situation and circumstance, in the midst of every company we keep. How would our life's journey of faith and discipleship to Christ be made stronger and richer if we acknowledged the presence of the eternally reliable, loving and grace-filled God. Perhaps we could begin our prayers in ways such as, **"Lord, may we notice You....."** or **"Lord, we know You are here; open our eyes to experience You...".**

✳ ✳ ✳ ✳ ✳ ✳ ✳ ✳ ✳ ✳

Reflections...

If you were trying to decide if someone was a follower of Christ, what evidence would you consider reliable to "convict" them of being a disciple of Christ?

Take a moment to experience Psalm 46:10-11: *"'Be still, and know that I am God! I am exalted among the nations, I am exalted in the earth.' The Lord of hosts is with us; the God of Jacob is our refuge."* Where do you see reliable evidence of God's presence and work around you?

Is there "reliable evidence" of your discipleship to Christ in your life?

36

Missing God...?

Again he said to them, "I am going away, and you will search for me, but you will die in your sin. Where I am going, you cannot come." Then the Jews said, "Is he going to kill himself? Is that what he means by saying, 'Where I am going, you cannot come'?"

He said to them, "You are from below, I am from above; you are of this world, I am not of this world. I told you that you would die in your sins, for you will die in your sins unless you believe that I am he."

They said to him, "Who are you?" Jesus said to them, "Why do I speak to you at all? I have much to say about you and much to condemn; but the one who sent me is true, and I declare to the world what I have heard from him."

They did not understand that he was speaking to them about the Father. So Jesus said, "When you have lifted up the Son of Man, then you will realize that I am he, and that I do nothing on my own, but I speak these things as the Father instructed me. And the one who sent me is with me; he has not left me alone, for I always do what is pleasing to him." As he was saying these things, many believed in him.   *- John 8:21-30, New Revised Standard Version*

Jesus continued, "I'm going away. You will look for me, and you will die in your sin. Where I'm going, you can't come." The Jewish leaders said, "He isn't going to kill himself, is he? Is that why he said, 'Where I'm going, you can't come'?"

He said to them, "You are from below; I'm from above. You are from this world; I'm not from this world. This is why I told you that you would die in your sins. If you don't believe that I Am, you will die in your sins."

"Who are you?" they asked.

Jesus replied, "I'm exactly who I have claimed to be from the beginning. I have many things to say in judgment concerning you. The one who sent me is true, and what I have heard from him I tell the world."

They didn't know he was speaking about his Father. So Jesus said to them, "When the Human One is lifted up, then you will know that I Am. Then you will know that I do nothing on my own, but I say just what the Father has taught me. He who sent me is with me. He doesn't leave me by myself, because I always do what makes him happy." While Jesus was saying these things, many people came to believe in him.   *- John 8:21-30, Common English Bible*

* * * * * * * * * *

"Can I find Jesus here?" The insistent young voice carried clearly over the bustle of children settling in for the opening of the first night of vacation Bible school, but Maggie was quickly distracted by the many tasks before her as the director. Excitement was in the air. Games, snacks, new friends, singing, even playing the bells had been promised, and **more than forty children were more than ready for the fun to begin!**

Finally the children were seated in their groups, and the vacation Bible school opening could begin. Maggie stepped up to the microphone at the front of the sanctuary and took a breath. Before she could get the first word out, a small hand waved insistently from the second row. **"Excuse me, lady? Can I find Jesus here?"**

Who IS that child? Maggie didn't recognize the little girl, but as she focused on the small, determined face, she knew she had to answer. **"Yes, sweetie, of course Jesus is here."** Maggie stepped back to the microphone, took a breath to speak, and….

"Where? Lady, if Jesus is here, where IS He?" This time, Maggie noticed tears welling up in the little girl's eyes, so she changed her plans. Calling to the music director, she asked, "Hey, Beth, would you come up here? I think we need to start with our theme song for this week. Would you come teach us?" Beth put down her papers and hurried to the front with her guitar as Maggie came down to sit with the little girl.

"Honey, Jesus is all over the place. He's here, and outside, and…well, everywhere God is, Jesus is too." The little girl started to cry. Maggie read her rainbow-shaped name tag. "Jamie, what's worrying you?"

"Well, my grandma told me we need God in our house, because it's all crazy and stuff, and I found out from my friend – that's her over there – that Jesus was God with skin on, and so if you could **just show me Jesus, I'll take Him home,** and then God will be in my house, and my daddy'll stop drinking and my brother will stop stealing grandpa's medicine and my mom will stop being so sad and crying all the time." Jamie took a big breath and pointed at the group of high school boys who were helping with vacation Bible school. **"So, which one is Jesus? Just tell me, please lady, and I'll take Him home, and then…..then God won't be missing any more. OK?"**

As the singing and clapping went on around them, Maggie sat with her arm around Jamie, wondering what she could say to reassure this little one who was facing such grownup issues. **"Jamie, God-sight isn't like people-sight, OK?** I mean, we know God is near when we see God at work around us, and in us too. God is here, and God is in your house too. **God isn't missing.** Maybe some people at your house are just not seeing God, that's all."

Jamie thought about that for a minute. Then, much to Maggie's relief, a smile appeared on her young face. "I get it! **We're people people, and Jesus is God people, and people eyes see different from God eyes, so God's here but my people eyes just can't see God, right?"**

Almost dizzy with following little Jamie's logic, Maggie nodded. "Yes, Jamie, so when you learn about following Jesus, and you act like Jesus is right there with you (because He is), then you'll find Jesus everywhere you go."

Later that evening, as the children were leaving after the closing songs, Maggie sat with Jamie as she waited for her mom to pick her up. Jamie looked up as the church doors opened. "That's my grandma!" She jumped up and ran to her grandmother. **"Guess what, grandma! I found Jesus, and He's coming home with us.** Isn't that amazing? God isn't lost, He's found, and you know what I learned at vacation Bible school? We're found too! Let's go home and find Jesus, grandma. Come on, let's go!"

And so it began. When Jamie's grandmother brought her the next night, the "snack ladies" invited grandma to help them, and she did. They invited her to come back each night and help. Each evening as they made and served snacks together, the ladies shared with Jamie's grandma how they saw God in their lives.

As those "snack ladies" came alongside grandma (Ruth), she felt a strength in her life she'd been missing for many years. When Jamie's brother died of a drug overdose, the church surrounded the family with care, prayer, and discipleship in action. One of the men, a recovering alcoholic, befriended Jamie's dad in his grief over losing his son, and led him to a recovery program which brought him to sobriety for the first time in over twenty years.

Missing? No, God was never missing. Jamie was quite right. Human eyes were the problem. Jamie knew (and would tell anyone who would listen!). God saw her all the time, she knew it. And God's eyes were the most important eyes!

* * * * * * * * * *

He said to them, "You are from below; I'm from above. You are from this world; I'm not from this world. This is why I told you that you would die in your sins. If you don't believe that I Am, you will die in your sins."

"Who are you?" they asked. Jesus replied, "I'm exactly who I have claimed to be from the beginning.

When we look around us at all the chaos in the world, **we can be so much like Jamie.** Where IS God, anyway? Our thoughts, and our voices are so much like the Psalm writer who says to God, *"Wake up! Bestir yourself for my defense, for my cause, my God and my Lord! (Ps. 35:23)* We get stuck. **We think that God is missing.** After all, how could the world be such a mess unless God was indeed missing?

Is it God, or is it our trust in God's never-failing presence which is missing? Jesus was, and is, exactly who He claimed to be from the start. Jesus, or as Jamie put it, "God with skin on", is always present. He sees us; He knows us; He loves us. **God is never missing, but sometimes we are.**

* * * * * * * * * *

Reflections...

How would you join in the kitchen conversation with grandma Ruth?

How have you experienced God's presence today? This week? This year?

Reflections (continued)

What would your family, neighborhood, community, world be like if everyone realized that God is indeed present in every place, every situation, always? What would change?

Young Jamie made an amazing difference in her family when she learned God was not lost, but was present in her home. What difference would believing that, and acting on that realization, make in your life?

37

Freedom: Stick to It!

Jesus said to the people who believed in him, **"You are truly my disciples if you remain faithful to my teachings. And you will know the truth, and the truth will set you free."**

"But we are descendants of Abraham," they said. "We have never been slaves to anyone. What do you mean, 'You will be set free'?"

Jesus replied, "I tell you the truth, everyone who sins is a slave of sin. A slave is not a permanent member of the family, but a son is part of the family forever. **So if the Son sets you free, you are truly free.** *Yes, I realize that you are descendants of Abraham. And yet some of you are trying to kill me because there's no room in your hearts for my message. I am telling you what I saw when I was with my Father. But you are following the advice of your father."*

"Our father is Abraham!" they declared."No," Jesus replied, "for if you were really the children of Abraham, you would follow his example. Instead, you are trying to kill me because I told you the truth, which I heard from God. Abraham never did such a thing. No, you are imitating your real father."

They replied, "We aren't illegitimate children! God himself is our true Father." Jesus told them, "If God were your Father, you would love me, because I have come to you from God. I am not here on my own, but he sent me. Why can't you understand what I am saying? It's because you can't even hear me! For you are the children of your father the devil, and you love to do the evil things he does. He was a murderer from the beginning. He has always hated the truth, because there is no truth in him. When he lies, it is consistent with his character; for he is a liar and the father of lies. So when I tell the truth, you just naturally don't believe me! Which of you can truthfully accuse me of sin? And since I am telling you the truth, why don't you believe me? **Anyone who belongs to God listens gladly to the words of God.** *But you don't listen because you don't belong to God."*

- John 8:31-47, New Living Translation

Then Jesus turned to the Jews who had claimed to believe in him. **"If you stick with this, living out what I tell you, you are my disciples for sure. Then you will experience for yourselves the truth, and the truth will free you."**

Surprised, they said, "But we're descendants of Abraham. We've never been slaves to anyone. How can you say, 'The truth will free you'?"

Jesus said, "I tell you most solemnly that anyone who chooses a life of sin is trapped in a dead-end life and is, in fact, a slave. A slave is a transient, who can't come and go at will. The Son, though, has an established position, the run of the house. **So if the Son sets you free, you are free through and through.** *I know you are Abraham's descendants. But I also know that you are trying to kill me because my message hasn't yet penetrated your thick skulls. I'm talking about things I have seen while keeping company with the Father, and you just go on doing what you have heard from your father."*

121

They were indignant. "Our father is Abraham!" Jesus said, "If you were Abraham's children, you would have been doing the things Abraham did. And yet here you are trying to kill me, a man who has spoken to you the truth he got straight from God! Abraham never did that sort of thing. You persist in repeating the words of your father."

They said, "We're not bastards. We have a legitimate father: the one and only God."

*"If God were your father," said Jesus, "you would love me, for I came from God and arrived here. I didn't come on my own. He sent me. Why can't you understand one word I say? Here's why: You can't handle it. You're from your father, the Devil, and all you want to do is please him. He was a killer from the very start. He couldn't stand the truth because there wasn't a shred of truth in him. When the Liar speaks, he makes it up out of his lying nature and fills the world with lies. I arrive on the scene, tell you the plain truth, and you refuse to have a thing to do with me. Can any one of you convict me of a single misleading word, a single sinful act? But if I'm telling the truth, why don't you believe me? **Anyone on God's side listens to God's words.** This is why you're not listening – because you're not on God's side."*

- John 8:31-47, The Message Version

* * * * * * * * * *

"You know, I couldn't wait to be free. Five years is a LONG time. I know I deserved it, but….I was so dumb. I thought all my problems would be over once I got done doing my time. This **freedom stuff is a lot harder than I thought.** It's tougher than I ever dreamed."

Ralph had been out of prison for three months when he shared those words with a support group for recently released inmates which was sponsored by a church in the community. That evening, we were thinking and sharing about what "freedom" meant.

Curt was listening a lot, but saying very little. He had finished his sentence just the week before. After fifteen years in prison, he described his "freedom experience" this way: "It's like the biggest jet lag I could imagine. I mean, **the world went on without me, and I'll never catch up. Ever."**

Ralph had served as one of the prison chaplain's assistants during his last two years of incarceration. "You know what gets me through? Let me see if I can find it…" He reached under his chair for his Bible and opened it to a place marked with a well-worn bookmark. "Here it is; listen and see what you think: '**If you stick with this, living out what I tell you, you are my disciples for sure. Then you will experience for yourselves the truth, and the truth will free you."** Here's the other one: '*Jesus said, "I tell you most solemnly that anyone who chooses a life of sin is trapped in a dead-end life and is, in fact, a slave. A slave is a transient, who can't come and go at will. The Son, though, has an established position, the run of the house. **So if the Son sets you free, you are free through and through.**'"*

Curt listened closely. "So what I hear you saying is, **freedom is a great gift, but sticking to it's the hard part. It that about it?"**

"Yep. You got it, Curt. Exactly. Our old ways felt like freedom, but we ended up stuck in thinly disguised slavery to death-dealing ways. Not freedom at all - in fact, it was the exact opposite. **Living in God's truth, following Christ, that's real freedom.** But here's the thing: some stuff in the world – you know what I'm talking about here, right? – that stuff will try to trick you into thinking God's freedom is inconvenient, a pain in the…well…you get it. But real pain? That happens when you don't claim the true freedom Christ offers you – and stick to it for all you're worth."

Curt nodded. "I get it. **It's what you stick to that defines who you are.** Sticking to this freedom Christ offers, that defines me as a truly free guy. That about it?"

Ralph smiled. "That's ALL of 'it'. No 'about' to it, Curt. Sticking to the freedom is ALL of 'it'!"

✳ ✳ ✳ ✳ ✳ ✳ ✳ ✳ ✳

Often the ways the world describes and defines "freedom" are quite different from the way Jesus defines it. **Many would say that "freedom" means the right to do what you want,** when you want, to whomever you want to do it to.

What Ralph, Curt, and many others throughout time have discovered is that **freedom defined in worldly terms is most times quite the opposite.** It is slavery - slavery to a self-centeredness which quickly takes over an entire life. This kind of deceptive "freedom" strangles joy and holy energy and replaces them with an insatiable ambition for personal gain and fame. Then all that's left is a hollow shell which might look good from the outside, but is really empty and dead on the inside.

Jesus calls his first followers, and us, to seek and stick to the true, rock-solid, eternal freedom He offers. This is not a surface "freedom show". **His freedom is deep down, soaked through and through, unshakable, unstoppable,...and eternal.**

I'll take that kind of freedom any day – and every day. How about you?

✳ ✳ ✳ ✳ ✳ ✳ ✳ ✳ ✳

Reflections...

What does the word "freedom" mean to you?

What comes to mind when you hear Jesus say, *"I tell you most solemnly that anyone who chooses a life of sin is trapped in a dead-end life and is, in fact, a slave. A slave is a transient, who can't come and go at will. The Son, though, has an established position, the run of the house. So if the Son sets you free, you are free through and through."?*

Reflections (continued)

Think about your life for the last week. Where can you spot the freedom Jesus speaks of?

If you can't identify this "through and through" freedom of Christ's at work in your life, what will you do about that?

38

A Life or Death Issue

The Jews answered him, "Are we not right in saying that you are a Samaritan and have a demon?"

*Jesus answered, "I do not have a demon; but I honor my Father, and you dishonor me. Yet I do not seek my own glory; there is one who seeks it and he is the judge. **Very truly, I tell you, whoever keeps my word will never see death.**"*

*The Jews said to him, "Now we know that you have a demon. Abraham died, and so did the prophets; yet you say, 'Whoever keeps my word will never taste death.' Are you greater than our father Abraham, who died? The prophets also died. **Who do you claim to be?**"*

Jesus answered, "If I glorify myself, my glory is nothing. It is my Father who glorifies me, he of whom you say, 'He is our God,' though you do not know him. But I know him; if I would say that I do not know him, I would be a liar like you. But I do know him and I keep his word. Your ancestor Abraham rejoiced that he would see my day; he saw it and was glad."

Then the Jews said to him, "You are not yet fifty years old, and have you seen Abraham?"

*Jesus said to them, **"Very truly, I tell you, before Abraham was, I am."** So they picked up stones to throw at him, but Jesus hid himself and went out of the temple.*   *- John 8:48-59, New Revised Standard Version*

The people told Jesus, "We were right to say that you are a Samaritan and that you have a demon in you!"

*Jesus answered, "I don't have a demon in me. I honor my Father, and you refuse to honor me. I don't want honor for myself. But there is one who wants me to be honored, and he is also the one who judges. **I tell you for certain that if you obey my words, you will never die.**"*

*Then the people said, "Now we are sure that you have a demon. How can you say that no one who obeys your words will ever die? Are you greater than our father Abraham? He died, and so did the prophets. **Who do you think you are?**"*

Jesus replied, "If I honored myself, it would mean nothing. My Father is the one who honors me. You claim that he is your God, even though you really don't know him. If I said I didn't know him, I would be a liar, just like all of you. But I know him, and I do what he says. Your father Abraham was really glad to see me."

"You are not even fifty years old!" they said. "How could you have seen Abraham?"

*Jesus answered, **"I tell you for certain that even before Abraham was, I was, and I am."** The people picked up stones to kill Jesus, but he hid and left the Temple.*   *- John 8:48-59, Contemporary English Version*

* * * * * * * * * *

After visiting someone in a hospital, I got lost trying to find my way back to the main entrance. I found myself in the oncology (cancer treatment) unit. Several patients were in the hallway. Some were walking, some in wheelchairs, and one on a rolling bed. The man lying on the bed said hello to me, so I returned the greeting.

As I started to pass by him, he asked me this question: **"So what IS life, anyway?"** I stopped, scrambling to find something helpful to say to this man lying on a rolling bed in the hallway of a hospital cancer treatment unit. He smiled, looked me straight in the eye, and repeated his question, **"So what IS life, anyway?"** I gave the first answer that came to me. "It's being able to make a difference, even in a small way, that spreads and magnifies God's grace and presence in the world."

He sighed. "Well, I suppose I can still do that, but probably not for long...**so what then?"**

I looked a bit closer. His physical body was reduced to skeletal form, but his eyes....his eyes glowed with a deep and compelling presence. "Well," I said, **"Then you get to experience real life. You'll be done with this introduction chapter and ready for the rest of the story. And that part lasts forever."**

He smiled. Tears of joy trickled from the corners of his eyes. **"I knew it! This can't be all there is. No way. It's all true then; real life is just beginning.** Thanks, my new friend. Thank you and thank you again."

No, I thought, *Thank YOU for the reminder.* What an amazing man I met that day.

* * * * * * * * *

Very truly, I tell you, whoever keeps my word will never see death."

I never learned the man's name. It really didn't matter. God spoke into my life that day with a reminder of true, eternal life priorities. **It really is a "life or death" issue.** If we live our lives as if this earthly life is all we've got, or it's the most important thing we have, we're missing the experience of true, real life. **Who would read the introduction of a book and then throw the rest away,** especially if the rest of the book was all about the experience of amazing, eternal grace and joy?

Jesus was issuing an invitation that day, an invitation to real, true life of eternal grace and joy with God. But they steadfastly insisted on clinging to the earthly portion of their lives as the most important. The rules and ways of believing and behaving also focused on, and prioritized, life's "introduction" so thoroughly that when the guide to heaven appeared in their midst they not only did not recognize Him, they repeatedly looked for ways to destroy Him. Yet even when they thought they'd succeeded, true, eternal life won.

When I met that man in the hallway, he reminded me: **"keeping the Word" means living our lives as if we're moving through the introduction here on earth toward the "rest of the story" in heaven with Him.**

In the end, true, eternal life always wins. And it really is...a life or death issue.

* * * * * * * * *

Reflections...

If you met the man in that hallway, how would you answer him?

Where is your life focused? Is the map of your life journey oriented towards true life, or are you stuck in the introduction?

39

Blinded by Illusions

As Jesus walked along, he saw a man who was blind from birth. Jesus' disciples asked, **"Rabbi, who sinned so that he was born blind, this man or his parents?"**

Jesus answered, "Neither he nor his parents. This happened so that God's mighty works might be displayed in him. While it's daytime, we must do the works of him who sent me. Night is coming when no one can work. While I am in the world, I am the light of the world."

After he said this, he spit on the ground, made mud with the saliva, and smeared the mud on the man's eyes. Jesus said to him, "Go, wash in the pool of Siloam" (this word means sent). So the man went away and washed. When he returned, he could see.

The man's neighbors and those who used to see him when he was a beggar said, "Isn't this the man who used to sit and beg?" Some said, "It is," and others said, "No, it's someone who looks like him."

But the man said, "Yes, it's me!" So they asked him, "How are you now able to see?"

He answered, "The man they call Jesus made mud, smeared it on my eyes, and said, 'Go to the Pool of Siloam and wash.' So I went and washed, and then I could see."

They asked, "Where is this man?"

He replied, "I don't know."   *- John 9:1-12, Common English Bible*

Walking down the street, Jesus saw a man blind from birth. His disciples asked, **"Rabbi, who sinned: this man or his parents, causing him to be born blind?"**

Jesus said, "You're asking the wrong question. You're looking for someone to blame. There is no such cause-effect here. Look instead for what God can do. We need to be energetically at work for the One who sent me here, working while the sun shines. When night falls, the workday is over. For as long as I am in the world, there is plenty of light. I am the world's Light."

He said this and then spit in the dust, made a clay paste with the saliva, rubbed the paste on the blind man's eyes, and said, "Go, wash at the pool of Siloam (Siloam means 'Sent'). The man went and washed – and saw.

Soon the town was buzzing. His relatives and those who year after year had seen him as a blind man begging were saying, "Why, isn't this the man we knew, who sat here and begged?" Others said, "It's him all right!" But others objected, "It's not the same man at all. It just looks like him."

He said, "It's me, the very one." They said, "How did your eyes get opened?"

"A man named Jesus made a paste and rubbed it on my eyes and told me, 'Go to Siloam and wash.' I did what he said. When I washed, I saw."

"So where is he?"

"I don't know."

- John 9:1-12, The Message Version

* * * * * * * * *

Overheard in a hospital hallway: **"Figure it out. Your little boy, he's sick because you two (pointing) didn't get married before you had him."**

"WHAT?"

Yeah. That's how it works. You sin. You pay."

"Really? So, tell me…what caused YOUR sickness?"

"What? **I'm not sick!**"

"Sure you are. Ignorance is a sickness. You know what I learned? See that nurse over there? She told us about the guy that Jesus told to stick spitty mud in his eyes. Jesus made that mud – get this – from the dirt of the world and part of Himself (his spit). Then He sent the guy to the pool (the nurse said it was the "Sent" Pool) to wash it all out. Guess what happened? Jesus beat the dirt of the world. Washed it right out. **So whatever the dirt is in your eyes, brain, wherever, let Jesus have it. Let Him spit all over it. You'll be amazed at the new vision you get. I was. And if there's hope for me, surely there's hope for you too. See ya."**

* * * * * * * * *

Life kicks up dirt and dust quite often, blurring our vision of the presence of Christ in our midst. Sometimes life spits on us (and worse), and we are blinded by the illusion that these struggles define our lives. We are literally overcome with dealing with the imperfections, pain, and realities of making it through one day at a time.

We can become as blind as the man Jesus met that day. We are blinded by the illusionary definition of life the world markets to us. We lose sight (literally) of the reminders and glimpses of heaven God shows us daily.

The presence of Christ is "mixed in" with the our life experiences every day. When we allow Him to wash and clear our vision (a daily spiritual practice, not a one-time thing), our lives gain new and powerful focus and strength. As we live daily in this way, we are truly "Sent" to demonstrate His amazing, grace-filled presence in the world – like the man who was born blind. We will discover new sight for true life, just as the dad in the hospital hallway did that day.

* * * * * * * * *

Reflections...

As you read the conversation in the true story above, what was your first reaction? Why do you think you reacted that way?

Now read the response of the boy's father again. How would you summarize what he said?

Think and pray: What "dust", "dirt", and "life-spit" is blurring and/or blinding you to the Lord's presence in your life today?

How can/will you let Christ wash the dust and dirt of the world out of your eyes so you can more clearly and powerfully see Him in the seasons and situations of your life?

40

What Do YOU Say?

They brought to the Pharisees the man who had formerly been blind. Now it was a Sabbath day when Jesus made the mud and opened his eyes. Then the Pharisees also began to ask him how he had received his sight. He said to them, "He put mud on my eyes. Then I washed, and now I see."

Some of the Pharisees said, "This man is not from God, for he does not observe the Sabbath." But others said, "How can a man who is a sinner perform such signs?" And **they were divided. So they said again to the blind man, "What do you say about him? It was your eyes he opened."** He said, "He is a prophet."

The Jews did not believe that he had been blind and had received his sight until they called the parents of the man who had received his sight and asked them, **"Is this your son, who you say was born blind? How then does he now see?"**

His parents answered, "We know that this is our son, and that he was born blind; but we do not know how it is that now he sees, nor do we know who opened his eyes. **Ask him; he is of age. He will speak for himself."** His parents said this because they were afraid of the Jews; for the Jews had already agreed that anyone who confessed Jesus to be the Messiah would be put out of the synagogue. Therefore his parents said, "He is of age; ask him."

- John 9:13-23, New Revised Standard Version

Then they took the man who had been blind to the Pharisees, because it was on the Sabbath that Jesus had made the mud and healed him. The Pharisees asked the man all about it. So he told them, "He put the mud over my eyes, and when I washed it away, I could see!"

Some of the Pharisees said, "This man Jesus is not from God, for he is working on the Sabbath." Others said, "But how could an ordinary sinner do such miraculous signs?" So **there was a deep division of opinion among them. Then the Pharisees again questioned the man who had been blind and demanded, "What's your opinion about this man who healed you?"** The man replied, "I think he must be a prophet."

The Jewish leaders still refused to believe the man had been blind and could now see, so they called in his parents. They asked them, **"Is this your son? Was he born blind? If so, how can he now see?"**

His parents replied, "We know this is our son and that he was born blind, but we don't know how he can see or who healed him. **Ask him. He is old enough to speak for himself."** His parents said this because they were afraid of the Jewish leaders, who had announced that anyone saying Jesus was the Messiah would be expelled from the synagogue. That's why they said, "He is old enough. Ask him."

- John 9:13-23, New Living Translation

* * * * * * * * * *

131

Ben and Mike had known each other since their days running on the high school track team together. Both young dads, these days their monthly fishing trips were more like twice-a-year getaways. As they sat on logs by the riverbank eating lunch, Ben asked Mike the question he'd been thinking about for months, ever since he'd found out that Mike's oldest boy Xavier had some kind of disease that would soon make him deaf.

"How can your boy be so happy? In another year, he'll be totally deaf. And yet when I asked him, he told me he'd already been healed. Said he could hear just fine – with his eyes. Sounds crazy to me! What's he talking about? How'd he get this 'healing' he talks about?"

Mike finished chewing and put his sandwich down. "Well, you know, I still struggle – a lot – with that one myself. But most days **Xavier calls it his 'new adventure', especially after that new family moved in next door to us. Their little girl Molly invited him to her 8th birthday party last month. Guess what she got for her birthday?"**

"Ya got me", Ben said, forgetting all about his own sandwich as he listened.

"She got a seeing eye dog. They even let her name him. Know what she calls him? 'See-Big'. That's his name. I thought it was a weird name, so I asked my boy about it. He laughed and told me Molly said See-Big was all about helping her see things with her whole self. **She said her grandma told her she'd probably never be cured, but with God's gift of See-Big, she could surely be healed.** Maybe it's all about that 'whole-self' thing."

Ben smiled. **"Sounds like it's all about a 'God-thing' to me.** That's what I'd say anyway."

Funny you should say that," Mike said. "That's exactly what Xavier said last night. Said he knows God's got big plans for him, just like He does for Molly. And I heard him telling his little sister Tilda that God gave Molly big ears and him big eyes, because God knew they'd need them. Last week the **docs told us Xavier'd probably completely lose his hearing** by this time next year. They started talking about so many options, implants, you name it….**my head started to spin!** Guess I looked pretty sad, because when the docs stepped out for a minute, my boy turned to me and told me – are you ready for this? – told me, **'Think big, Dad, REAL big, OK?'"**

Ben's mouth fell open as he remembered something. "That's exactly what our track coach used to say before every meet, especially the ones we were sure we'd lose – big. I'll never forget. Every time any of us passed by Coach Dale, he'd say it: 'Think big. Don't ever forget, son, think BIG'. **How'd your son know that saying so well?** You use it with him?"

Mike smiled and shook his head. "Nope, never said that to him, ever. **This just has to be a God-thing,** like Molly said. Because when I heard those words come out of Xavier's mouth, **I knew it was God talking to me through him.** So I'm thinking big. I'm looking for big. I'm dreaming big. And I know for a fact, that whatever happens with his hearing, **Xavier's already healed."**

* * * * * * * * *

"They asked them, 'Is this your son? Was he born blind? If so, how can he now see?' His parents replied, 'We know this is our son and that he was born blind, but we don't know how he can see or who healed him. Ask him. He is old enough to speak for himself.'

Nelson Mandela, South African anti-apartheid leader and former national leader, said it well:

"Our deepest fear is that we are <u>not</u> inadequate. Our deepest fear is that we are powerful beyond measure. It is our light, not our darkness that most frightens us. You are a child of God. Your playing small does not serve the world. There's nothing enlightened about shrinking. We were born to make manifest the glory of God that is within us. It is not just in some of us; it is in everyone. And as we let our light shine, we unconsciously give other people permission to do the same."

We are old enough to speak for ourselves. No one of us is cured of all the ailments, afflictions, and struggles in our lives, but when we celebrate, demonstrate, and communicate the many "God-things" in our lives, we are healed beyond measure.

What do YOU say?

* * * * * * * * *

Reflections...

Each of us is blind in some way(s). If we open ourselves to the grace and healing available to us as we follow Christ, He will open our eyes every bit as powerfully as He did for the "man born blind".

Think of a struggle in your life that you have been able to overcome. How did you overcome it? Can you see the action of God in the overcoming? What do you say?

Think of those whom God has placed in your life: family, friends, coworkers, neighbors, acquaintances. How is (or could) God use you to bring a voice or touch of healing to them? What do you say?

41

Sight Beyond Sight

The leaders called the man back and said, "Swear by God to tell the truth! We know that Jesus is a sinner." The man replied, "I don't know if he is a sinner or not. **All I know is that I used to be blind, but now I can see!"**

"What did he do to you?" they asked. "How did he heal your eyes?" The man answered, "I have already told you once, and you refused to listen. **Why do you want me to tell you again? Do you also want to become his disciples?"**

The leaders insulted the man and said, "You are his follower! We are followers of Moses. We are sure God spoke to Moses, but we don't even know where Jesus comes from."

"How strange!" the man replied. "He healed my eyes, and yet you don't know where he comes from. We know that God listens only to people who love and obey him. God doesn't listen to sinners. And this is the first time in history anyone has ever give sight to someone born blind. Jesus could not do anything unless he came from God."

The leaders told the man, "You have been a sinner since the day you were born! **Do you think you can teach us anything?" Then they said, "You can never come back into any of our synagogues!"**

- John 9:24-34, Contemporary English Version

They called the man back a second time – the man who had been blind – and told him, "Give credit to God. We know this man is an impostor." He replied, "I know nothing about that one way or the other. **But I know one thing for sure: I was blind...I now see."**

They said, "What did he do to you? How did he open your eyes?"

"I've told you over and over and you haven't listened. **Why do you want to hear it again? Are you so eager to become his disciples?"**

With that they jumped all over him. "You might be a disciple of that man, but we're disciples of Moses. We know for sure that God spoke to Moses, but we have no idea where this man even comes from."

The man replied, "This is amazing! You claim to know nothing about him, but the fact is, he opened my eyes! It's well known that God isn't at the beck and call of sinners, but listens carefully to anyone who lives in reverence and does his will. That someone opened the eyes of a man born blind has never been heard of – ever. If this man didn't come from God, he wouldn't be able to do anything.

They said, **"You're nothing but dirt! How dare you take that tone with us!" Then they threw him out in the street.**

- John 9:24-34, The Message Version

* * * * * * * * *

Several months ago, **I spent the morning with a lady spending her second day in her new home – a skilled nursing facility in a nearby town.** She was a bit confused, but more despondent than anything else. She told me she felt **abandoned, useless, and worthless.** After her family left to get some lunch and pack some of the things she wanted to bring to her new home, Mabel turned to me, tears in her eyes. **"Why won't God just call me home?** Why do I have to spend time in this awful way-station on the way there?"

"Excuse me?" A voice came from the other side of the curtain in the room. A couple seconds later, the curtain opened. "Did I hear right? Is your name Mabel? Mine's Phyllis. Don't mean to interrupt, but I've been waiting all morning to say hello. You came in late yesterday, and I knew you'd be tired, so I just kept to myself over here the best I could."

Mabel managed a smile that didn't quite reach her eyes. "Hello, Phyllis. **So did your kids put you here too? Maybe we can put our heads together and figure a way out –** you know like in the movies, a jail break or something...something..." Her smile disappeared as tears threatened to overflow her eyes.

Phyllis scooted her wheelchair closer. "I haven't been here that long either – maybe a week. I lose track of time these days. And the answer to your question is, **I put me here. I just thought I was too much of a burden on my grandson.** He's such a good boy, but he's got a wife and three kids (I was a great grandma again just a few weeks ago!). They told me I'd never be a burden, but I could see differently. Anyway, when I heard you use the 'jail' word...that rang a bell with me."

Mabel snapped back, **"Well, lucky you to have family who wanted to keep you.** So what kind of bell you got ringing over there? Your hearing aids going funny or something?"

Phyllis got serious. "Nope, believe it or not, don't need 'em. My hearing's just fine. Just can't see too well's all. And I keep getting weak in the knees and falling. Anyway, back to that 'jail' thing. All I know is, this place used to feel like a jail to me too, but now it's different. It's really about seeing beyond what you think you see. **I learned something from a little girl named Cathy who came here with her church group to sing to us.** Had all kinds of braces and crutches, she did. She was all interested in my wheelchair, **told me she had 'ceebal polly'** and she'd probably need a chair like mine someday."

Phyllis had both Mabel's and my attention as she took a deep breath and continued. "Her mom came with the group too. She told me Cathy had cerebral palsy. When I remarked about how hard it must be for little Cathy, her mom smiled. She said her little girl was her inspiration because it was all about possibilities, not limitations, with Cathy. What made all the difference to me was when she told me this: **'Cathy refuses to be imprisoned by limitations – absolutely refuses. That frees her to see amazing possibilities that the rest of us often miss.** Cathy has taught me this is truly a new life. It's not about 'can't'; it's all about what we can do – with God's amazing grace and help.'"

Mabel shook her head and rolled her eyes. **"Oh, that 'Jesus stuff', right?** Well, if He set so many prisoners free, I want Him to give me the key to this place too, so I can escape! Really though, tell me the truth. What really changed your mind so much about this place?"

Phyllis scooted a bit closer. "Mabel, why do you keep asking? Do you really want to see beyond what you think you see? That's where real freedom is, you know..."

That conversation began a wonderful friendship. When I visited again a couple of months later, I found Mabel and Phyllis laughing and sharing a Bingo playing card in the activities area as a church group led the monthly "Bingo Night". **Together, these two women were daily discovering their God-given "sight beyond sight".**

* * * * * * * * *

One of my favorite responses from those touched by Jesus comes from this man healed of his blindness:

All I know is that I used to be blind, but now I can see!"   *"What did he do to you?" they asked. "How did he heal your eyes?" The man answered, "I have already told you once, and you refused to listen.* **Why do you want me to tell you again? Do you also want to become his disciples?"**

Those who challenged this man had him in his place: the blind guy. They refused to understand that Jesus had truly set him free. They had imprisoned him in his blindness, but they were in fact the ones who were truly blind. The newly-seeing man knew that **true vision – the sight beyond sight** – came not so much from restoration of physical sight, but more accurately and completely **from discipleship to Christ.**

Mabel couldn't see beyond her "imprisonment" in the skilled nursing facility. Before she met Phyllis, she was blinded by her limitations. She was blind to the many possibilities present in her new home, her new reality of life. **Phyllis, almost physically blind, was able to use her "sight beyond sight" to overcome the limitations,** thus freeing her for new life. The day they met, she in effect asked Mabel the same question, "Do you also want to become His disciple?". In other words, **"Do you really want true sight, sight that will see you through this life season to victory?"**

Mabel's answer was "yes". What's yours?

* * * * * * * * * *

Reflections...

Think about your life. Is anything "imprisoning" you? Perhaps it's emotional or spiritual entanglements, failures, temptations. Maybe this is just a tough season of life for you financially, physically, in relationship(s). Are you more focused on the limitations, or the possibilities?

The limitations were still there for Mabel (her family still didn't want her) and Phyllis (she was still legally blind, and losing even more sight). But they learned more each day to see beyond the limitations to the new possibilities. **Their lives were forever changed by Phyllis's conversation with a little girl one day.**

What does little Cathy have to say to you in your life today?

42

Real Blindness – True Sight

When Jesus heard what had happened, he found the man and asked, "Do you believe in the Son of Man?"
The man answered, "Who is he, sir? I want to believe in him."
"You have seen him," Jesus said, "and he is speaking to you!"
"Yes, Lord, I believe!" the man said. And he worshiped Jesus.
Then Jesus told him, **"I entered this world to render judgment-- to give sight to the blind and to show those who think they see that they are blind."**
Some Pharisees who were standing nearby heard him and asked, **"Are you saying we're blind?"**
"If you were blind, you wouldn't be guilty," Jesus replied. "But **you remain guilty because you claim you can see."**
- John 9:35-41, New Revised Standard Version

Jesus heard they had expelled the man born blind. Finding him, Jesus said, "Do you believe in the Human One?"
He answered, "Who is he, sir? I want to believe in him."
Jesus said, "You have seen him. In fact, he is the one speaking with you."
The man said, "Lord, I believe." And he worshipped Jesus.
Jesus said, **"I have come into the world to exercise judgment so that those who don't see can see and those who see will become blind."**
Some Pharisees who were with him heard what he said and asked, **"Surely we aren't blind, are we?"**
Jesus said to them, **"If you were blind, you wouldn't have any sin, but now that you say, 'We see,' your sin remains."**
- John 9:35-41, Common English Bible

* * * * * * * * * *

The two neighbors watched as the **police led the young man next door out to the waiting patrol car.** Maybe finally the constant stream of visitors (day and night) would stop. Florence had lost track of how many times she'd called the cops about the suspicious around the clock visitors next door. As she and her housemate Carol sat on the front porch watching, Florence found herself thinking out loud.

"Wonder where they're taking him…he looks young. Think he's eighteen? Such a shame….such a waste…"

Carol had no doubts, and spoke right up. **"Oh, I know where HE's going…straight to Hell. Anybody can see that!"**

"Really?" Florence wasn't so sure.

Carol was incredulous. **"It's as plain as day. How could you miss it?"**

Florence shook her head, a thoughtful look on her face. "Hmmm…I don't know about that. What I do know is, **sometimes my vision's not as good as I think it is."**

"What?" Carol couldn't believe her ears. Why, just a year ago Florence's 15 year old grandson had lost his life to a drug overdose!

Florence's next words stunned Carol into silence…and thoughtfulness. She said, **"We're all blind to something…what we need is some true sight – some "Jesus-vision"."**

Later that evening, as the neighbors on the other side of the young man's house were passing by on their evening walk, Carol went out to say hello. "Hi Bonnie. Hello Todd. Did you see the action next door? **The cops finally came and got that drug-dealing guy and took him away. Good thing, too. Don't need his kind around here.** We all know where he's going to end up, don't we?" Carol was talking so fast that it took her a minute to see the confused look growing on both Bonnie and Todd's faces.

"You mean young Max? They took Max?" As Bob spoke, Carol was surprised to see how upset he was. Connie seemed just as concerned. **"Why? Max was a good kid.** Did they put him in cuffs and everything? Where were they taking him?"

Just then, Florence came out to join the conversation. "No, Bonnie. I didn't see any handcuffs, and we don't know for sure what's going on. Do you know the young man?"

Todd spoke up. "We certainly do. He was living with his dad in Nevada, but then his dad got real sick. Cancer, I think. Anyway, **his dad died a couple weeks ago,** and a few days ago Max came here to live with his mom. Trouble is, **mom and her boyfriend, and whoever else they had living there, they pulled out of here last week.** Max came knocking on our door, but we couldn't tell him anything. We've been helping him out. Come on, Bonnie. We need to make some calls. **He's only seventeen years old, and he's alone in this mess. We can't have that. No way."** He pulled his cell phone out and began dialing as he walked away.

As Bonnie turned to follow her husband, she had these last words for Carol: **"Watch out for those blind spots, Carol. They've messed with my true sight many a time. Always go for God's true sight;** watch out for what the world shows you, because a lot of times that's what'll make you blind. We'll let you know what happens." And Bonnie hurried to catch up with Bob.

Carol learned a lot that week. She gained a lot of the "true sight" Florence told her about. Todd and Bonnie took Max under their wing and cared for him through all the turmoil of that season of his young life. They helped him celebrate his eighteenth birthday the following month (Florence and Carol baked an amazing birthday cake), and the men's group at Todd's church helped Max clean out his mother's house. Bonnie helped Max get enrolled in the local community college, and the same men's group pulled their resources together to encourage and assure Max he could pursue his dream of being a registered nurse someday.

Carol wasn't the only one to gain "true sight". **Max discovered just how powerful and life-changing "Jesus-sight" could be** through the words and actions of an amazing group of new friends and God-given new family.

From real blindness…to true sight – simply amazing!

* * * * * * * * *

We are often so swift to accept what we see at first glance, often so fast to accept (and pass judgment) on what we first hear and experience. The world around us can (and often does) blind us to the true sight God seeks to give us each moment of every day.

Jesus was offering true sight to the Pharisees that day, but they were blind (really blind) to the vision He sought to give them. **They were blinded by their own sight,** their own assumptions, their own definition of reality (pretty limited), their own judgment.

It's so easy for us to fall into the same trap they did....

＊ ＊ ＊ ＊ ＊ ＊ ＊ ＊ ＊

Reflections...

Put yourself in Carol's place for just a moment. Can you understand her assumptions and reaction? Why (or why not)?

If you could tell Max something, what would it be? How would what you say demonstrate "true sight"?

43

Hey! Can You Hear Me NOW?

*"I tell you the truth, anyone who sneaks over the wall of a sheepfold, rather than going through the gate, must surely be a thief and a robber! But the one who enters through the gate is the shepherd of the sheep. The gatekeeper opens the gate for him, and the **sheep recognize his voice and come to him. He calls his own sheep by name and leads them out.** After he has gathered his own flock, he walks ahead of them, and **they follow him because they know his voice. They won't follow a stranger; they will run from him because they don't know his voice."***

*Those who heard Jesus use this illustration didn't understand what he meant, so he explained it to them: "I tell you the truth, **I am the gate for the sheep.** All who came before me were thieves and robbers. But the true sheep did not listen to them. Yes, I am the gate. **Those who come in through me will be saved. They will come and go freely and will find good pastures.** The thief's purpose is to steal and kill and destroy. **My purpose is to give them a rich and satisfying life.***

- John 10:1-10, New Living Translation

*"Let me set this before you as plainly as I can. If a person climbs over or through the fence of a sheep pen instead of going through the gate, you know he's up to no good – a sheep rustler! The shepherd walks right up to the gate. The gatekeeper opens the gate to him and **the sheep recognize his voice. He calls his own sheep by name and leads them out.** When he gets them all out, he leads them and they follow because they are familiar with his voice. They won't follow a stranger's voice but will scatter because they aren't used to the sound of it."*

*Jesus told this simple story, but they had no idea what he was talking about. So he tried again. "I'll be more explicit, then. **I am the Gate for the sheep.** All those others are up to no good – sheep stealers, every one of them. But the sheep didn't listen to them. I am the Gate. **Anyone who goes through me will be cared for – will freely go in and out, and find pasture.** A thief is only there to steal and kill and destroy. **I came so they can have real and eternal life, more and better than they ever dreamed of."***

- John 10:1-10, The Message Version

* * * * * * * * * *

It was just a small, run-down looking cabin next to the barn. If you weren't looking (and didn't already know it was there), you'd probably miss it. But to anyone "traveling the rails" in the cold Michigan winter, that small cabin was a slice of heaven.

It intrigued me the first time I saw it. I'd stopped at the roadside produce stand on the country road to see what they were selling. As I walked to the end of one of the tables, there it was – in plain sight not fifty yards in front of me.

140

The hand-lettered sign on its door intrigued me. It read simply, "The Jesus Gate".

So I asked the lady selling fruits and vegetables about it. She smiled. "Want a tour? It's quite a place. My husband built it with his dad in memory of the people who used to live here." Before I could stop her, she called out to her husband, **"Hey Mike! Come show this lady the Little Jesus House."**

As we walked across the yard to the little cabin, I never would have guessed how this tour would change my perception of the passage of Scripture quoted above. As we passed through the doorway (labeled "The Jesus Gate"), **the beauty of the walls inside almost took my breath away.** As Mike turned the lights on, amazing wall murals came to life. Looking from the doorway around the one-room cabin, on all four walls, the words of John 10:1-10 were written and illustrated.

As my mouth fell open (as I know it did), Mike smiled. **"My dad, he "rode the rails", as they say. Life dealt him a bad hand, he told me so many times, but God changed all that when he got off the train here one day.** See, the folks who owned the big house here heard his story, and they took him in. They prayed with him right there on the big house porch, then they moved him into this little cabin. It was pretty run down then, not at all what you see now. My dad started working for them, so when the original cabin here started to fall apart, they took him into the main house. When he found a bride, they took her in too. When they had me, why, **I never knew till I was a teenager they weren't my real grandparents!"**

As I continued to gaze in amazement of the beautiful artwork on the cabin walls, Mike continued his story. "When they got so they couldn't keep the place up, they went to live with one of their kids and **deeded the whole place to my dad...for a dollar.** That just about gave dad a heart attack. They gave it to him that way on one condition: He had to promise to do his best to **show anybody passing through the same "Jesus-Gate" they'd shown him years before.** He promised, and he kept his word."

When Mike got married, he and his new wife Marilou settled in with his now-aging dad. They tore down the old cabin and built a new one. It was then **Mike learned something about his dad he never knew.** His dad was a very talented artist. One day a few months after his mom's death, he got worried because hadn't seen his dad in hours. He looked all over the property, and what he saw when he finally decided to check out the cabin almost took his breath away. He discovered his dad painting the first of the wall murals.

As father and son sat amid the painting in progress, his dad finally told him his life story. **Mike learned about all the "Jesus-Gates" God had opened in his dad's life.** Dad's instruction, "This here's your heritage, son. Here's where my life changed. This is what gets passed on. Not all the ugly before it; none of that gets through these gates without being changed by Him. Nothing. **Can you hear me now, son?"**, got a committed "Yes, sir!" from Mike that day.

As we got ready to leave the cabin, Mike pointed to the inscription over the doorway going out. "I painted that the day I came back from Dad's funeral. **It's not as good as Dad's stuff, but somehow I think he'll understand. It's my way of telling him that I surely do hear him now.**

I looked up and read these words as we left the cabin: **"Take the Pasture, and the Shepherd, with you!"**

I heard him, loud and clear. And I do believe I did just that. I took it with me that day, and the next, and...

* * * * * * * * *

Many times we find ourselves "riding the rails" of life. On and on we go, not sure of where we're really headed. Day by day, time flies, faster and faster. We lose sight of what (or who) is guiding us. We just keep moving, on and on. We fail to notice the many invitations of Christ to His pasture to be fed, renewed, refreshed, and guided in the pathway to true Life.

Over and over, it's as if we can hear Jesus say to us, "Can you hear Me....NOW?" Time and time again, the Shepherd calls us in so many ways. "Can you hear Me...NOW?" The amazing thing is that once we hear Him, each time we do, it gets easier to hear His voice. Soon, we develop the habit of tuning into the Shepherd of our life's voice. Then one day we realize that among all the voices competing for our attention in life, it is His that overpowers them all. It's His voice we tune into automatically.

Soon, our answer to His "Can you hear Me now?" is a repeated, **"Of course I can. You are my Shepherd!"**

May it always be so.

* * * * * * * * * *

Reflections...

Read the Scripture at the beginning of this chapter again. Why do you think it spoke so powerfully to Mike's dad?

How would you describe "riding the rails of life"?

In what ways do you hear the voice (or sense the presence) of Jesus, the Shepherd, in your life?

44

When the Wolves Come

*"I am the good shepherd. The good shepherd lays down his life for the sheep. **The hired hand, who is not the shepherd and does not own the sheep, sees the wolf coming and leaves the sheep and runs away-- and the wolf snatches them and scatters them.** The hired hand runs away because a hired hand does not care for the sheep.*

*"I am the good shepherd. I know my own and my own know me, just as the Father knows me and I know the Father. And **I lay down my life for the sheep.** I have other sheep that do not belong to this fold. I must bring them also, and they will listen to my voice. So there will be one flock, one shepherd.*

*"For this reason the Father loves me, because **I lay down my life in order to take it up again. No one takes it from me, but I lay it down of my own accord.** I have power to lay it down, and I have power to take it up again. I have received this command from my Father."*

Again the Jews were divided because of these words. Many of them were saying, "He has a demon and is out of his mind. Why listen to him?" Others were saying, "These are not the words of one who has a demon. Can a demon open the eyes of the blind?" - John 10:11-21, *New Revised Standard Version*

*"I am the good shepherd, and the good shepherd gives up his life for his sheep. **Hired workers are not like the shepherd. They don't own the sheep, and when they see a wolf coming, they run off and leave the sheep. Then the wolf attacks and scatters the flock.** Hired workers run away because they don't care about the sheep.*

*"I am the good shepherd. I know my sheep, and they know me. Just as the Father knows me, I know the Father, and **I give up my life for my sheep.** I have other sheep that are not in this sheep pen. I must also bring them together, when they hear my voice. Then there will be one flock of sheep and one shepherd.*

*The Father loves me, because **I give up my life, so I may receive it back again. No one takes my life from me. I give it up willingly!** I have the power to give it up and the power to receive it back again, just as my Father commanded me to do.*

The people took sides because of what Jesus had told them. Many of them said, "He has a demon in him! He is crazy! Why listen to him?" But others said, "How could anyone with a demon in him say these things? No one like this could give sight to a blind person!" - John 10:11-21, *Contemporary English Version*

* * * * * * * * * *

As I attended a big dog show some years ago, I met a veteran shepherd in the food concession area. As I settled down at the end of one of the long tables in the central eating area, we struck up a conversation. His

143

nametag read "Brice", and I soon learned that he was one of the judges at the show's sheep herding trials. I also learned he had amazing, real-life shepherding stories to share.

"You know," he began, **"We could all learn a lot from old Shep here...an awful lot.** Save us a lot of trouble in life it would too, if we'd just pay some attention to the teachin'" It wasn't until he pointed under the table that I noticed **a beautiful, gray-in-the-muzzle Australian shepherd.** Shep's tail thumped and he raise his head at the sound of his master saying his name. Then he settled in at Brice's feet for story time.

I introduced myself and settled in to listen. He said, "Yep. **You see those sheep over there? They belong to Shep. They know him, and he knows them. Well. Very well.** They know his smell, how he moves, what he looks like, everything about him."

Wow. I nodded and kept listening.

Brice continued. **"And he knows them.** What they look and smell like. How they move. What they need. And real important - **he knows what tempts them most.** One other thing about Shep: **He would die for them."** He looked up from his food straight into my eyes. "And he did almost die for them once..."

That was the day I heard about wolves. Real wolves and spiritual wolves – both with sharp teeth, big appetites, and destructive habits. Brice told me about the time before he got Shep when thieves stole half his flock one night. They thought they'd killed his dog, named Right Hand, but the faithful sheepdog managed to crawl to the back door. The dog's whining woke Brice, and he'd opened the door to discover his dying sheepdog just as he heard the engines of the sheep thieves speeding away from his place. "That was the day the spiritual wolves came," he said. "I just about gave it all up that day. That flock, I had over a hundred sheep. Those lambs and that wool was my bread and butter. Without them, I didn't know's I'd make it."

He paused to take a bite, and I had to ask. **"So what changed?** When did you get Shep?"

Brice smiled. "Well now, **that's a real sheep and shepherd story.** You see, **I learned a big lesson that day. I'm a sheep too.** God not only knows my name and everything about me, stuff even I don't know; **God has provided a rock-solid Shepherd for me too.** He knows what I look like, how I smell, what I need most....and what tempts me to stray. He knows it all. **When my human wolves came, I found my Shepherd.** He guided me to the safest, most amazing life pasture I could ever have imagined. And then there was Shep."

As Brice paused again for a bite of food, I realized I'd forgotten all about the food on my plate. The food I was getting through the old shepherd next to me was far more attention-getting.

He took a drink and then went back to his story. "A week or so went by. The one day when I was sort a feelin' sorry for myself again, I heard a big truck engine coming up my drive. Well, **they're not gonna get the rest of my sheep, no sirree, so I grabbed my shotgun and took off out my door to greet 'em proper.** But when I saw what was coming, I just about fell over. Any guesses?"

Nope, by then I had no good guesses...

He smiled. "Well, it was the sheriff's truck....hauling a trailer with my sheep in it! **Seems they caught the thievin' human wolves who stole 'em, and there was a bonus in it for me.** Sheriff Rick said to me, he said, 'Found this pup with your sheep. Little guy, but if you want to give him a home, he's yours.' That's how I got old Shep there. Sheriff told me something else too. See my big ram over there? He's onry as all get-out. Sheriff said when he tried to get hold of puppy Shep the first time, that old ram blocked him every which way – just put his old horned head down and glared at him. So **you betcha Shep'd die for them.** See those scars on his side? Shep got those just last year defending his sheep. He 'bout died keepin' them safe; yes he did indeed." He bent down and scratched Shep between the ears, and Shep thumped his tail again.

* * * * * * * * *

Brice knew a lot about herding sheep. He thought he knew a lot about life in general. **But when the wolves came,** Brice learned something that would take him through all life's valleys and challenges, struggles and temptations. Brice claimed his place in the flock of Christ's disciples; **he met his Shepherd in one of the deepest, darkest valleys of his life.** That Shepherd led him to strength and safety and showed him abundant grace which would see him through the rest of his days.

* * * * * * * * *

Reflections...

What "human wolves" have you seen around you lately? Perhaps you have some prowling in your own life, or the life of someone you know.

Shep (and the old ram) are examples that taught Brice what it meant to point not just himself, but others he met toward the true Shepherd, Jesus the Christ. What examples like them have you seen or experienced?

45

Holy Voice Recognition

The time came for the Festival of Dedication in Jerusalem. It was winter, and Jesus was in the temple, walking in the covered porch named for Solomon. The Jewish opposition circled around him and asked, "How long will you test our patience? If you are the Christ, tell us plainly."

*Jesus answered, "I have told you, but you don't believe. The works I do in my Father's name testify about me, but you don't believe because you don't belong to my sheep. **My sheep listen to my voice. I know them and they follow me. I give them eternal life. They will never die, and no one will snatch them from my hand. My Father, who has given them to me, is greater than all, and no one is able to snatch them from my Father's hand. I and the Father are one."***
- John 10:22-30, Common English Bible

They were celebrating Hanukkah just then in Jerusalem. It was winter. Jesus was strolling in the Temple across Solomon's Porch. The Jews, circling him, said, "How long are you going to keep us guessing? If you're the Messiah, tell us straight out."

*Jesus answered, "I told you, but you don't believe. Everything I have done has been authorized by my Father, actions that speak louder than words. You don't believe because you're not my sheep. **My sheep recognize my voice. I know them, and they follow me. I give them real and eternal life. They are protected from the Destroyer for good. No one can steal them from out of my hand. The Father who put them under my care is so much greater than the Destroyer and thief. No one could ever get them away from him. I and the Father are one heart and mind."***
- John 10:22-30,The Message Version

* * * * * * * * * *

Picture this situation: It's Friday night, and two teenage girls, one whose parents are away for the weekend, the other whose single dad is working overtime and won't be home until very late, are making plans for evening entertainment...

Now listen in to this conversation:

"Nope. Not doing that. Not going there. Ever. No way."

"Come ON, Jody, why not? It'll be so much FUN!"

"Ah…no. And no. LaShaunda, I don't hear the voice of anything good in that. Not even a whisper of good there."

"Seriously? You're not going to come out with that Jesus stuff again, are you? Come on, Jody, please? Just this once? Fun, Jody, FUN…**It is Friday night; you did notice that, right?"**

"You asked, so here's all I'll say about that. **I <u>know</u> the voice of the one <u>I</u> follow**, and this is definitely not it. **It's like a built-in voice recognition program.** It got installed the day I was baptized, and I'm telling you – I don't follow what I don't recognize. And I'm for sure not recognizing that voice in what you're inviting me to. But I will surely pray for you. You can count on that."

"You sure, girlfriend? You're gonna miss out big time. Troy and his friend Tyrone are going to be there, and they are HOT! **Last chance….see me walking out the door….."**

"Just remember,…girlfriend – that installation I was talking about? It's free. You really should look into that; it'll save you a lot of grief, like what you're maybe walking into tonight. But no, not doing that, not going there. Ever."

"OK, Jody; gave you the chance. See ya."

Four hours later the ringing phone woke Jody up. Caller ID said it was LaShaunda, but when Jody answered, it wasn't her friend…

"Hello, Miss? This is County General Hospital. Can you help us? We need you to identify the owner of the phone I'm calling you from." *What?*

It was the call no one wants to receive. Jody's loud, "Oh my God!" woke up her dad, who had just fallen asleep in his room down the hall. As he came rushing in, he found her jumping into her jeans and jamming her feet into her flip flops. Tears streaming down her face, he heard her tell the caller, **"We'll be right there. Oh my God. My dad's coming with me. Oh my God!"**

LaShaunda went to the party. It was no party for her. Sexually assaulted, she was dumped in the woods outside town. A clerk on her way home from work at the hospital found her stumbling along the road. When she stopped her car to help, LaShaunda fell into her arms sobbing and then passed out as the woman helped her into the car. As she shut the car door, the woman noticed a scratched, beat up cell phone on the ground, so she took it to the hospital along with the injured and unconscious girl.

Jody and her dad arrived at the hospital and were directed to LaShaunda's room. The police officer stationed outside the door was waiting for them. "You Jody?" Her dad answered, "Yes, this is Jody, and I'm Jody's dad. Is LaShaunda going to be OK? I've called her parents; they're out of state, and they're coming home as fast as they can."

The officer looked at Jody. **"Miss, we need your help here. LaShaunda keeps saying something strange.** Over and over, she asks for you, then she babbles **something about needing some kind of voice recognition program … says Jody knows how to install it, and she needs it.** The docs think she'll be OK, but does any of this make sense to you?"

"Yes ma'am, it does. Can I go see her? I think I can help with that." Jody's dad caught on fast, and he smiled. "Oh yes, officer, I think this will surely help our young patient. **It'll be the best medicine she ever gets."**

That evening, LaShaunda was baptized in her hospital room shower. And what she now calls her **"Holy Voice Recognition program"? It's been working just fine ever since.**

* * * * * * * * *

My sheep recognize my voice. I know them, and they follow me. I give them real and eternal life. They are protected from the Destroyer for good. No one can steal them from out of my hand. The Father who put them under my care is so much greater than the Destroyer and thief. No one could ever get them away from him. I and the Father are one heart and mind."

We who are older than these young ladies can perhaps shake our heads as we read about this situation. **We'd never fall for this sort of thing...or would we?** Maybe it's not an ill-conceived party which tempts us to follow other guiding voices in our lives. Perhaps it's.......or maybe ....

Jody understands. **As her life seasons change, the Tempter's voice will change too.** But if she continually grows in her discipleship, if she keeps her spirit and mind fed with prayer, Scripture, worship, Christian community, **that "holy Voice Recognition" program** she shared with her friend LaShaunda will be a powerful life-saving force in her life. Someday, it **will guide her straight to her eternal home, where she will meet the Owner of that Voice – face to face.**

* * * * * * * * *

Reflections...

What tempting "voices" compete with the voice of God for attention in your life?

What's the state of your "Holy Voice Recognition program"?

46

Stoning....GOD?

Once again the people picked up stones to kill him. **Jesus said, "At my Father's direction I have done many good works. For which one are you going to stone me?"**

They replied, "We're stoning you not for any good work, but for blasphemy! You, a mere man, claim to be God."

Jesus replied, "It is written in your own Scriptures that God said to certain leaders of the people, 'I say, you are gods!' And you know that the Scriptures cannot be altered. So if those people who received God's message were called 'gods,' why do you call it blasphemy when I say, 'I am the Son of God'? After all, the Father set me apart and sent me into the world. Don't believe me unless I carry out my Father's work. But if I do his work, believe in the evidence of the miraculous works I have done, even if you don't believe me. Then you will know and understand that the Father is in me, and I am in the Father."

Once again they tried to arrest him, but he got away and left them. *He went beyond the Jordan River near the place where John was first baptizing and stayed there awhile. And many followed him. "John didn't perform miraculous signs," they remarked to one another, "but everything he said about this man has come true." And many who were there believed in Jesus.*   - John 10:31-42, New Living Translation

Again the Jews picked up rocks to throw at him. **Jesus said, "I have made a present to you from the Father of a great many good actions. For which of these acts do you stone me?"**

The Jews said, "We're not stoning you for anything good you did, but for what you said – this blasphemy of calling yourself God."

Jesus said, "I'm only quoting your inspired Scriptures, where God said, 'I tell you – you are gods.' If God called your ancestors 'gods' – and Scripture doesn't lie – why do you yell, 'Blasphemer! Blasphemer!' at the unique One the Father consecrated and sent into the world, just because I said, 'I am the Son of God'? If I don't do the things my Father does, well and good; don't believe me. But if I am doing them, put aside for a moment what you hear me say about myself and **just take the evidence of the actions that are right before your eyes. Then perhaps things will come together for you, and you'll see that not only are we doing the same thing, we <u>are</u> the same – Father and Son. He is in me; I am in him."**

They tried yet again to arrest him, but he slipped through their fingers. *He went back across the Jordan to the place where John first baptized, and stayed there. A lot of people followed him over. They were saying, "John did no miracles, but everything he said about this man has come true." Many believed in him then and there.*
                    - John 10:31-42, The Message Version

* * * * * * * * * *

The children sat quietly, entranced by the story the talented storyteller wove during the Children's Welcome time in Sunday morning worship. **Mr. Bontee's retelling of the Scripture passage quoted above had the sanctuary so quiet** that the sound of the air conditioners on that hot July morning could be clearly heard.

As he finished the story, and Jesus escaped the clutches of His would-be killers safely, there were quite a few sighs of relief (and not just from the children up front). Then a small but insistent voice accompanied a raised hand among the children.

"But Mr. B, why would they want to kill Jesus…with rocks?" As the young girl's voice broke with sadness, Mr. Bontee was clearly struggling to find a good and comforting answer. Before he could respond, another child, and then another, and another, supplied these powerful words:

"I know! I know! **Because if they let Him really <u>be</u> Jesus, they couldn't be the biggest bosses any more. They were <u>scared</u>…"**

"They sure were scared. They were just big bullies, that's what they were. **And everyone knows that bullies are just the scared-est people around. I think they were real stupid – thinking they could kill God.** Ha! And He got away from them every time, especially when they thought they really killed him. That came later, Mr. B, right? God really showed 'em that time!"

"Whoohoo! That last time was the best ever. **He surprised 'em all with his escape that time. Then He came back and showed 'em all. And He's right here right now too. Right, Mr. B?"**

Mr. Bontee started clapping, and soon applause echoed through the sanctuary. The pastor came down from her seat to where the children were gathered and asked the children to please stand.

She said, **"Friends, let's recognize our preachers of the Word this morning.** You have heard the Word proclaimed and taught by God today through the lips of these children and their blessed storyteller. Lord, we thank You for the gift these Your children have brought us from Your throne of grace this morning. May we all be blessed and guided this day by what you have made known through them. And all God's people said a loud and sure….."

The responsive "Amen!" echoed powerfully through the congregation gathered that day as the children were invited to remain up front for prayer and Communion time. At the end of worship, the pastor invited them to stand with her for the benediction prayer, **"May each one of us truly live the reality that Jesus did indeed conquer, not only those who tried to kill him, but those who thought they had destroyed Him. Let's live the resurrection!"**

And the children danced and bounced down the center aisle of the sanctuary with the pastor to a chorus of "Amen!" from the gathered congregation.

* * * * * * * * * *

If we look around today, we can see attempts to "stone Jesus" in many places and situations. The children in worship that day were very insightful – and correct. **We really do want to be in charge of our own lives.** We pretend that we are in essence "self-made people". When godly priorities compete with our desires and we choose what we want to think, say, and/or do over that which we know Christ is guiding us toward, we in effect throw a rock at Him, driving Him back (but never away).

For just when we think we've "won", Christ shows us He will never give up on us – ever. Do what we will, we cannot kill Christ. He will come to life again. Resurrection power rules!

* * * * * * * * *

Reflections...

Why do you think the people that day wanted to kill Jesus?

Go back and read the responses of the children once more. How would you respond to each child?

Can you think of an instance where a life choice could in essence be described as trying to "stone Jesus"? What is it?

How could a different choice be made in that instance, which would instead demonstrate Christ's resurrection power?

Appendix 1

Bible Translations and How to Find Them

Five versions/translations of Scripture are used in the Exploring... Bible study series. One or more of them may have appealed to you as you read and experienced this book. You may wonder what's different about them. You may have decided you'd like to purchase one or more.

The information contained here should assist you in doing just that. Here is a brief description of each version/ translation along with sources, should you decide to purchase one or more of them.

Contemporary English Version, published by the American Bible Society (ABS) in 1995, is available through them (www.bibles.com). Originally intended as a children's translation, it uses very simple, contemporary language which can be read and easily understood by those of all ages. The CEV is one of the versions recommended especially for those for whom English is a second language. The New Testament was translated directly from the Greek text; Psalms and Proverbs from the Masoretic Hebrew text; and the balance from their original languages as well.

New Revised Standard Version, published in 1989 by the National Council of Churches, is an updated version of the Revised Standard Version. The NRSV is available in most Christian and large volume bookstores, as well as from the American Bible Society (www.bibles.com). It is the most widely used ecumenical (used by many Christian traditions) version and is used in many seminaries. A committee of about thirty members of various Protestant denominations and the Roman Catholic Church participated, as well as Jewish and Eastern Orthodox participants for the Old Testament.

Common English Bible, published by Cokesbury, is available from many sources, including cokesbury.com and amazon.com. You can explore this translation further online at www.commonenglishbible.com. Here are two reviews of this fairly new translation:

"The Common English Bible, likely the largest cross-denominational translation project in recent memory, unites Baptist, Catholic, Evangelical, United Methodist, and numerous other faith traditions in a joint effort to create a complete but broadly accessible Bible for the 21st century. No single translation, despite the breadth of this committee's reach, is likely to please all, but this sincere and diligent effort goes far toward the creation of a plain-English version that, without falling into folksiness or false hipsterism, can be read and understood by a range of ages, educational backgrounds, and aptitudes." (Library Journal, March 2011)

"It is a rare and wonderful thing when undisputedly strong scholarship and reader accessibility come together, and yet that is exactly what has happened in this new and altogether impressive translation of the scriptures, the Common English Bible. You will find yourself reading certain passages as if for the first time. I highly commend the CEB to scholars, students, and seekers alike who want to explore the richness of God's Word in a fresh way." (The Rev. Canon C. K. Robertson, Ph.D.)

New Living Translation, published by Tyndale House Publishers in 1996, is available from many sources, which include Christian bookstores, large 'regular' bookstores, and online resources such as the American Bible Society (www.bibles.com). Bible Gateway (www.biblegateway.com) describes the NLT this way: "The goal of any Bible translation is to convey the meaning of the ancient Greek and Hebrew texts as accurately as possible to the modern reader. The New Living translation is based on the most recent scholarship in the theory of translation. The challenge for the translators was to create a text that would make the same impact in the life of modern readers that the original text had for the original readers. In the New Living Translation, this is accomplished by translating entire thoughts (rather than just words) into natural, everyday English. The end result is a translation that is easy to read and understand and that accurately communicates the meaning of the original text."

The Message, published by NavPress / Eugene Peterson, can be obtained at many Christian bookstores as well as 'regular' large bookstores. The Message can also be ordered through its own website: www.messagebible.com. It is described by the publisher as follows: "Why was *The Message* written? The best answer to that question comes from Eugene Peterson himself:

"While I was teaching a class on Galatians, I began to realize that the adults in my class weren't feeling the vitality and directness that I sensed as I read and studied the New Testament in its original Greek. Writing straight from the original text, I began to attempt to bring into English the rhythms and idioms of the original language. I knew that the early readers of the New Testament were captured and engaged by these writings and I wanted my congregation to be impacted in the same way. I hoped to bring the New Testament to life for two different types of people: those who hadn't read the Bible because it seemed too distant and irrelevant and those who had read the Bible so much that it had become 'old hat.'

Peterson's parishioners simply weren't connecting with the real meaning of the words and the relevance of the New Testament for their own lives. So he began to bring into English the rhythms and idioms of the original ancient Greek—writing straight out of the Greek text without looking at other English translations. As he shared his version of Galatians with them, they quit stirring their coffee and started catching Paul's passion and excitement as he wrote to a group of Christians whom he was guiding in the ways of Jesus Christ. For more than two years, Peterson devoted all his efforts to *The Message New Testament*. His primary goal was to capture the tone of the text and the original conversational feel of the Greek, in contemporary English.

Some people like to read the Bible in Elizabethan English. Others want to read a version that gives a close word-for-word correspondence between the original languages and English. Eugene Peterson recognized that the original sentence structure is very different from that of contemporary English. He decided to strive for the spirit of the original manuscripts—to express the rhythm of the voices, the flavor of the idiomatic expressions, the subtle connotations of meaning that are often lost in English translations.

The goal of *The Message* is to engage people in the reading process and help them understand what they read. This is not a study Bible, but rather "a reading Bible." The verse numbers, which are not in the original documents, have been left out of the print version to facilitate easy and enjoyable reading. The original books of the Bible were not written in formal language. *The Message* tries to recapture the Word in the words we use today."

The Common English Bible, published by_____

Appendix 2

Notes

All stories contained in this book are true. Names and identifying characteristics have been altered, except where persons have given permission to be identified.

About the author

Rev. Dr. Al W. Adams is an ordained pastor in the Christian Church (Disciples of Christ) tradition. She has served in many and varied locations and ministries, which have included hospital and police chaplaincy, congregational leadership, and church planting. Trained in coaching and mediation, she has also served as consultant, mentor, and seminar leader/facilitator for clergy, congregations, and leadership teams. Her passion is bringing individuals and congregations together as Scripture and faith come alive in them, thus enabling them to be and do more than they dare ask...or imagine! (Eph. 3:21) Dr. Al has a BS in Education and a Masters degree in counseling from the University of Missouri, a Masters of Divinity (M.Div.) from Eden Theological Seminary in St. Louis, and a Doctor of Ministry (D.Min.) from Brite Divinity School (Texas Christian University). This is the first book in the 'Exploring...Everyday Stories' series of Bible studies and preaching stories.

The Exploring Series is more than just a great Bible study. Rev. Al has combined her knowledge of the scripture with her gift of telling real life stories to make the scriptures come alive. This series will challenge you to grow in your Everyday journey to intimacy with Christ as you gain deeper understanding of the scriptures. I look forward to each new study and recommend this book to everyone who wants to deepen their walk of faith

> Deb Martin, Deskside Support Specialist, large IT outsourcing company,
> Love's Foundation Christian Church, Brighton, CO.

I really enjoy the Exploring series. The series works so well as a Bible study program or as a jump off point for an in-depth discussion. I have used several of these meditations for our staff devotions over the last few years, and they have sparked some great discussions. The stories that pertain to the readings are wonderful, thought provoking, funny, serious, and at times sad. I highly recommend reading and using these nuggets of truth in your life.

> Jane Fleischer, St. Luke's Episcopal Church, San Antonio, TX.

I am an old Christian but a new Christian in study of the Bible. Pastor Al has given me new insight into the message the Bible gives to each of us. I LOVE her stories. They speak to my heart, and they provide wonderful images for my mind to mull over. I have a new way to start my prayers with God. As one of the stories says, "Hello Love"- I know God smiles.

> Sue Aggson, member, United Methodist Church, Fort Morgan, CO

www.ingramcontent.com/pod-product-compliance
Lightning Source LLC
Chambersburg PA
CBHW081329090426
42737CB00017B/3066